"Beautiful, wise, tender, and true."

CHERYL STRAYED, #1 NYT bestselling author *Wild*

"Powerful and beautiful. Fans of *The Last Lecture* (2008), by Randy Pausch, or *Motherless Daughters* (1994), by Hope Edelman, will appreciate the authors' navigation of grief with monumental and unforgettable courage."

BOOKLIST

"Written by a mother-daughter duo, the two of them share their sides and experiences of their changing relationship after it is revealed that the mother has terminal cancer."

Seventeen **"17 Books Every Girl Should Read Before She's 17"**

"As someone who lost my mom at the same age Marisa did, and to the same villain—cancer—*The Goodbye Diaries* is a sermon, a heartfelt duet, and a meditation; on mother- and daughter-hood, on unconditional love, and on the painful liberation of letting go. It is a triumph."

JOY-ANN REID, journalist and MSNBC anchor of "AM Joy"

"Moms and daughters share a powerful bond. This emotional mother-daughter memoir chronicles the journey of a terminal cancer diagnosis and gives readers a heartfelt, honest glimpse of the experiences that unite us through it all."

Better Homes & Gardens **"11 Books We Can't Wait to Read in 2019"**

"A stunning tribute to a remarkable relationship, further proof that love lives on beyond life itself."

HOPE EDELMAN, NYT bestselling author of *Motherless Daughters*

"What both authors share is an obvious love for one another, and the diary approach demonstrates that in ways big and small, letting them discuss their love of trips to The Gap together or their family jokes about *Seinfeld* alongside heart-to-heart talks about the future. That relationship carries the book—a lovely tribute to a dedicated mother."

FOREWORD REVIEWS

"As a specialist in teen girls, I found *The Goodbye Diaries* deeply touching in its spot-on expression of the nuances that character-ize mothers and daughters in what I see as the most sacred yet complex relationship of all relationships. A smart and moving read that inspires the reader into clarity and gratitude for the preciousness of love and its transcendence beyond loss."

LUCIE HEMMEN, PHD, psychologist, author of
The Teen Girl's Survival Guide

"Marisa Bardach Ramel has written a gorgeous book. It's less of a story about loss, and more about life and the bonds that bring us together. This book should be required reading for anyone facing the death of a loved one."

CLAIRE BIDWELL SMITH, *The Rules of Inheritance*

"This book grabs me by the throat. Reading a mother's thoughts and experiences, juxtaposed to a daughter's, is wholly evocative and searing. Readers will eagerly come along for Ramel's explo-sive and heart-wrenching ride."

ALLISON GILBERT, *Passed and Present*

"Sure to engage and enlighten mothers and daughters everywhere, and any reader who has ever loved and lost."

SARAH SAFFIAN, *Ithaka: A Daughter's Memoir of Being Found*

"I know it could not have been easy to share such a personal story. It is a welcome addition to my collection."

JIMMY CARTER, 39th President of the United States

"*The Goodbye Diaries* is engrossing, frank, heartbreaking, and, ultimately, inspiring. This remarkable dual memoir is far more than the sum of its parts: it's not just the story of a mother and a daughter, but also of their unforgettable relationship, which would prove stronger than any of the devastating surprises life had in store for them."

WILL SCHWALBE, NYT bestselling author of
The End of Your Life Book Club

"In this deeply moving memoir, tight-knit mother-daughter duo Marisa Bardach Ramel and the late Sally Bardach share their experiences of coping with Sally's terminal cancer diagnosis in the last months of her life. Though it's a memoir about grief and loss, it's also as much a tribute to the unbreakable bonds between mothers and daughters."

Real Simple

"This emotional memoir, written by Marisa Bardach Ramel and the late Sally Bardach, chronicles the relationship between mother and daughter as they struggle to reconnect in the wake of a terminal cancer diagnosis. While that may sound grim, it's ultimately a heartwarming and inspiring story about how powerful the mother-daughter bond can be."

Good Housekeeping

the
Goodbye Diaries

the
Goodbye Diaries

A Mother-Daughter Memoir

Marisa Bardach Ramel
and Sally Bardach

Wyatt-MacKenzie Publishing
DEADWOOD, OREGON

The Goodbye Diaries
A Mother-Daughter Memoir

Marisa Bardach Ramel and Sally Bardach

ISBN: 9781948018364, Softcover
Library Congress of Control Number: 2019932302

Cover design: Mark Ramel.
Cover photo: Gloria Dawson + iStock. Author photo: Melissa Thornton.

Some permissions pending until final publication.

The Goodbye Diaries is a work of nonfiction. Some names and identifying details of people described in this book have been changed to protect their privacy.

The author gratefully acknowledges permission to reprint from the following publications: A version of "The Dress" was published as "The Perfect Prom Dress" in *Chicken Soup for the Soul: Thanks to My Mom* ©2015 and was reprinted in *Chicken Soup for the Soul: Thank You, Mom* bookazine, 2018. Chicken Soup for the Soul, LLC. All rights reserved. It was also reprinted as "Prom Dress Shopping with Two Months to Live" on *The Huffington Post* ©2015.

Portions of "Go Go Go" were published as "My Mom Died 10 Years Ago, But How Am I Supposed to Choose a Wedding Dress Without Her?" on *xoJane* ©2014 and appear courtesy of Say Media Inc.

Wyatt-MacKenzie Publishing
DEADWOOD, OREGON

Published by Wyatt-MacKenzie Publishing
info@wyattmackenzie.com

Marisa

To my great aunt, Ruth Sweedler,
who mothered the motherless.

And to my mother, Sally.

Sally

To Shirley,
my first roommate in the hospital.

And to Bill, Jordan, and Marisa.

AUTHOR'S NOTE

If we've learned anything as a society in recent years, it's that emotional memories stick. Although my mother was diagnosed with cancer in the year 2000—nearly twenty years ago—that period of time is carved into my heart. The wound is not fresh, but the memories of it are.

Thankfully I did not have to rely on memory alone. This book is pieced together from chapters my mother and I wrote, an almost-ridiculous number of journal entries, my mother's medical notebooks, and interviews with family and friends who generously helped fill in the gaps.

Everyday life continues when someone you love is sick, and certain relationships greatly affected my experience of my mother's illness. In some instances, to protect the privacy of those who crash-landed into my life during this time, I've changed names, altered identifying characteristics, approximated dialogue, or created composite characters. However, their impact on our story remains the same.

Marisa Bardach Ramel

CONTENTS

Foreword

I first met Marisa Bardach Ramel in 2014 at the Lustgarten Foundation's Pancreatic Cancer Research Walk in Long Island, NY. As President & CEO of the Lustgarten Foundation, the nation's largest private funder of pancreatic cancer research, I meet thousands of patients, survivors, and loved ones on our walks each year.

When Sally was diagnosed in 2000, pancreatic cancer research was practically non-existent—despite the fact that it was the nation's fourth leading cause of cancer deaths (it's now the third). Sally was passionate about the Lustgarten Foundation's mission to find a cure. Sally wanted to be part of the movement, even if it would be too late for her, so she attended our inaugural walk in 2001 with Marisa's father and brother. Eighteen-year-old Marisa chose not to go because that's what teenagers do—instead of dealing with complicated emotions like grief, they avoid it.

More than a decade later, Marisa finally felt ready to participate in the walk, and was surprised to find it uplifting. She participated again and again, most recently with her father, stepmother, husband, toddler son and infant daughter, warmed by the powerful bond that still connects her to Sally and that she hopes to experience with her own daughter.

Although Marisa and I met because of Sally's diagnosis, *The Goodbye Diaries* is not a book about pancreatic cancer. Rather, it is a beautifully written, heartwarming, and at times even humorous memoir about the ups and downs of mother-daughter relationships. It's an honest account of both Marisa's and Sally's most raw, uncensored emotions as they both confront futures they had never imagined possible. Told in alternating voices, Sally and Marisa offer their unique perspectives on what it's like to know you're leaving your loved ones behind, and what it's like to know you must navigate your life without your mother—your rock and best friend.

Teenagers and young adults will relate to this authentic story of a teenager's difficulty in processing how she will survive without her mother—an experience more terrifying than any imaginable adolescent angst. Especially for any young person who has a parent with a life-threatening or terminal illness, Marisa's story validates and gives voice to their deepest fears: What will happen to me when I can't run to my mom with every little problem like I once did? How will I get through so many life milestones like graduation, my wedding day, and the birth of my children without my mom by my side?

Mothers will relate to Sally's fierce determination to reconnect with her daughter. Adolescence tends to separate even the closest parents and children, as our once affable kids suddenly retreat to their rooms without even a hello—let alone throwing a terminal diagnosis into the mix. Hearing about Marisa's internal struggles gives perspective and insight to even the most well-intended parents, while Sally's spirit, patience and love for her daughter will inspire parents to hang in there, even on their toughest days.

For anyone who knows someone experiencing a life-altering event, this book is a must-read. I lost my mom to cancer, and I know firsthand that even as an adult, you are never prepared for that day—

whether you're twenty or fifty. Reading this book reminded me that the mother-daughter bond is never broken and while I will never stop missing her, it made me reflect on and cherish the many special moments we shared.

The Goodbye Diaries is a gift for Marisa's two children who will never know their grandmother Sally, and a treasure for everyone who reads this book. You will be reminded to appreciate your parents and your children every day, to not sweat the small stuff, to always say I love you, and to give that extra hug. For all parents who eventually have to let their kids leave the nest, this book will give you faith that you did your best, and now it's their turn to live and be the best person they can be. I can only imagine that Sally is beaming with pride about the value and comfort this book will bring to other families.

Kerri Kaplan
President & CEO
Lustgarten Foundation
Woodbury, New York

Prologue

I t's too good to be true.

This is my worry when I become pregnant in the first month of trying. This is my worry when the first ultrasound at five weeks is too early to detect the heartbeat. This is my worry as the first trimester drags on, a miscarriage looming every day. My mom's second pregnancy ended at twelve weeks, so won't mine, too? Aren't all of her things now mine—not just her clothing and jewelry, not just her smile and figure, but her deadly genes for miscarriage and cancer and heartbreak?

My anxiety only intensifies when the doctor confirms what I know in my soul: it's a girl.

How could it not be too good to be true? It is a storybook ending. Fifteen years after my mom dies, I not only find a publisher for our book, but I'm gifted a daughter. And that's what she feels like: a gift sent from my mother, and her mother, and all my ancestors in the great beyond.

Except instead of feeling thankful, I fret. I wonder how I will ever finish my book edits before she arrives, and work tirelessly throughout the pregnancy instead of letting my body rest. I grow anxious that she'll be born super early, then even more anxious when at thirty-eight weeks she's still firmly inside.

In our tiny Brooklyn apartment, I prep the bassinet, the infant car seat, the bouncy chair, the activity mat. I wash burp cloths and sterilize bottles and pacifiers. I place her tiny socks in the drawer alongside my toddler son's. The logistics are peaceful, then panic-inducing. By preparing, I worry that I'm jinxing her arrival, certain I will become just another mom on Facebook posting about my little girl who never was. *And she lost her mother, too,* friends will murmur, sending heart emojis as I mourn my one chance at reviving the relationship I lost.

In the middle of the night, I imagine dying during childbirth. I fear leaving my children too early, the way my mom left us. How helpless I'll feel to see from above my grief-stricken husband and toddler and newborn and know I can do nothing to comfort them. How helpless my mother must feel still. In the morning I look at photos from when I was born, snuggled safely in my mother's arms, and wonder if that first embrace is a promise or a lie.

On the outside, I am the stock image of a happy pregnant woman. On the inside, I am still a grieving daughter. In some ways, you never stop being the age you were when your mother died. That makes me frozen at twenty. Not still a kid, but not yet an adult, and simultaneously craving to be both.

Fifteen years has changed some things, though. At twenty, I thought I was the only young person who'd been dealt a bad hand. At thirty-five, I'm old enough to know that everyone gets their share of hardship. Yet I waver between relief that I've filled my quota, and worry that I should brace for the next impact. I live each moment with my family as if they're our last, and not in that sunshiney Hallmark way. It's more like looking at the world through nostalgia-tinted glasses: an intense pressure to transfer each moment into a memory, filed for later when my loved ones are gone. If my family knew how many eulogies I've composed for them in my head, they'd probably stop hanging out with me.

And yet, for each eulogy, there's a birth announcement. The birth of a book my mother and I began writing together nearly two decades ago, when she was first diagnosed. Forever I'll remember her phone call at midnight and her conspiratorial whisper: "Missy, let's write a book." Even now, when I edit our chapters, I feel her hands guiding mine across the keyboard, as light and powerful as those upon a Ouija board. And then, of course, there's the "real" birth: the any-day-now arrival of my baby girl and the mother-daughter relationship born anew. It's both a blessing and a burden. I fear I'll try too hard to replace the relationship I still miss, that I'll try to make us Sally and Marisa instead of letting us be who we will be. I worry that her every tiny move, both beautiful and hurtful, will have the power to reopen the wounds of my grief.

As the weather changes to spring, I point out flower buds to my son, and a sprig of hope grows within me. What if I just let myself be happy? Couldn't it be too good to be true, and yet be both good *and* true?

My daughter reassures me from the inside with an Olympic gymnast tumble, the way she has throughout my pregnancy. The seismic shift in my belly leaves me in awe. *She never makes me worry,* I say to friends about her acrobatics. And yet, by her mere presence, and the fear of her absence, she makes me worry all the time.

She quiets down. Resting a hand on my stomach, I caress a leg or an arm, who knows which, and imagine my little girl brightening up the spaces left dark by my grief. And I wait.

Marisa Bardach Ramel
May 1, 2018

CHAPTER 1

Diagnosis

Marisa / Sally

As a kid, I hated Saturday nights. It was date night. Mom and Dad went out to dinner and a movie and paid my brother, Jordan, $20 to babysit me. After hugs I hung on to for too long; after shouts of "love you" and "be good" and "set the alarm!"; after the front door shut behind them with a finality I dreaded, I'd linger at the living room window. Watching their car as it trailed down the block, I'd swipe back my babyish tears. It didn't matter how old I was: nine, ten, eleven. Whenever my parents went out, I was sure I'd never see them again.

I didn't consider how they would die. It was more like a disappearing act. Some magical force would sweep over them and—poof—they would vanish.

It didn't happen quite that way (nothing ever happens the way you think). But part of that fear, a child's worst nightmare, came true on a white-sky winter day—January 13, to be exact. One minute my parents were scolding me about my "pigsty" room, and the next Mom was dying.

———

When I show up at Mom's bed, I just give her a look, and she automatically scoots over to make room for me. Tonight I curl up beside her, and she tucks her faded brown blanket around us. I breathe. Sometimes it feels like an exhale of the day—my gossipy Long Island high school, the senior year stress of who I'll take to prom and where I'll go to college, and something boy-related, always something boy-related. Mom knows not to ask; she just lets me be.

To take my mind off things tonight, Mom tells me a story she's told me a million times. I don't really mind. Mom and I balance each other that way. She loves to talk, and I love to listen.

The story is about her mother, Grandma Rose, who died when I was a baby. Mom says her mother was her best friend, and that, after her mother died, Mom was even more grateful to have me—her little girl. "You'll always be my best friend, Missy," she says.

Mom pauses expectantly. She's waiting for me to say, "You're my best friend, too, Mom." I love this story, but I hate this part—the pressure to say it, the guilt if I don't. I used to say it when I was younger, but now I'm not a little girl anymore. I'm seventeen.

"Mo-om," I say, rolling my eyes and giggling.

"I know, I know, Laura's your best friend—and she's a wonderful friend," Mom says, reading my mind. "But one day you'll see. There's nothing like the mother-daughter bond."

She smiles knowingly, like she can see into the future, and I relax and nestle against her. Soon I'm going to graduate and go away to college, but for now I allow myself to have moments like this. A reprieve from all the thoughts swirling around in my head.

My parents' room is my nightly escape. I always know what I'll find: the lamp turned to the second-dimmest setting, an empty mug of Lemon Soother tea on the bedside table, and Mom sitting up in bed reading a library book—which, when I come in to chat, she spreads facedown on Dad's side of the bed. He'll be up soon, now that he's done watching *The Simpsons* in his comfy chair in the den downstairs. Sometimes he laughs so hard at that show—one big, loud "Ha!"—that I hear him from my bedroom on the second floor. It always makes me smile. I hear Dad put the last few dishes into the dishwasher, and I try to motivate myself to get up.

I hug Mom goodnight, and Dad ruffles my hair as we pass on the stairs. Our house is a heavily-trafficked split level, with Mom and Dad on the top floor, Jordan and me in neighboring rooms on the second floor, and the rest of our house on the first floor. Tonight I slip into my room to call Tony, the singer of the punk band I joined last month. I was shocked when I tried out to play drums and they picked me. But even more surprising are Tony's nightly phone calls, which started off about the band and now are just to talk. He called during dinner tonight and when I call him back he tells me there's a Battle of the Bands coming up in a few months, and we talk about whether I can learn all their songs by then. Somehow it turns into us making fun of all the dumb stereotypes about girl drummers, and I'm cracking up. He's so funny and easy to talk to, not like my boyfriend, Wilson, where I'm always nervous we'll run out of things to say.

Hours later, hanging up with a smile lingering on my face, I sneak downstairs to the computer in the living room to chat online with Wilson. We've been together ten months, but long distance for five, ever since he went away to college in Pittsburgh. The guys in my grade who ran track with him always ask me how he is, starry-eyed as if they're asking about a celebrity. I think they fell in love with the same things I did. His sweetness. His gentleness. His shyness. His wide smile—once you see it, you just want to make it reappear. Because he's so painfully shy, we mostly talk online. I don't mind. At least then, emboldened by the Internet, he eventually types the three words I long to see: I miss you. I wait for him to write it, stay up as long as it takes. I don't know if it's the distance, or his quietness, or just me being a girl, but I need the reassurance. Only then do I finally pass out.

I regret staying up so late when my alarm goes off at 6 a.m. the next day. "Four hours is not enough sleep for a growing girl," Mom nags. Which doesn't even make sense because I'm five-foot-two and ninety pounds, and haven't grown in years. And Dad gets annoyed because I hit snooze a million times and he has to yell down to my room to make sure I'm getting up. Eventually he pounds on my door, and then I rush out of bed to get ready in ten minutes flat.

I'm standing at the kitchen counter, scarfing down a bowl of cereal and glaring at the clock because I have to leave in three minutes or I'm going to be late for Calc, when Mom comes downstairs. Everyone says we're identical, with our petite frames and big smiles. It doesn't help that our outfits often match. Today it's the jeans we bought last week at Marshalls paired with crew-neck sweaters—turquoise for her, army green for me. I borrowed her sweater and even washed my hair this morning because I'm seeing Wilson after school. He's home on winter break, so we finally get to go on a date. When we first started going out last year—he a cool senior, me a smitten junior—we thought it was funny to dress up and go to Burger King for strawberry milk shakes and chicken nuggets. Now that he's in college, we've upgraded to a local pizzeria.

"Don't you look beautiful!" Mom says, coming over to touch my long curls. She pulls her hand away like she's been shocked. "Missy, you can't go out like this. It's twenty degrees, and your hair is sopping wet."

"Mom, *stop*," I grumble through sloshy cereal bites, swatting her away. "It's fine."

"It's January," she says, as if I don't know. She opens the cabinet and reaches for a bowl, pouring cereal for herself. "You're already run down—you'll get sick."

"I don't have time to blow-dry it."

"Well, if you woke up when your alarm went off, you would."

"It's not my fault! I'm tired."

"Then you shouldn't stay up 'til 2 a.m. talking on the computer!"

"Ugh! Are we done yet?"

"No," she shoots back, then takes a breath and looks at me. "Listen, Daddy and I won't be home right after work today. I have an appointment with the stomach doctor."

"OK," I say, glad they'll be gone and off my back, adding, "I'm having dinner with Wilson anyway," a tinge of smugness in my voice.

Mom continues, as if she didn't hear me: "He thinks it might be something with my pancreas."

I stop shoveling my cereal and look at her. What the hell does she mean, her *pancreas*? I don't even remember where it is or what it does—my brain rewinding to ninth-grade Bio and drawing a blank—but I'm pretty sure it's high up on the list of organ importance.

"What do you mean?" I ask. My voice sounds shakier than I want it to.

"I don't know," she admits, fussing nervously with the cardboard closure of the cereal box. Looking up, she sees my worried face and shoots me a bright smile. "We'll see what the doctor says."

"OK," I say, but my body won't budge. I want to ask more, or say something nice, but I can't figure out what. I look at the clock. "Oh God, I'm so late."

I slam my bowl into the sink and rush upstairs to brush my teeth, grab my messenger bag, and give myself one final look in the mirror. A serious reflection stares back at me. *Her pancreas?* Mom's always been a hypochondriac, so when she started having back pain last year I wasn't concerned. She's fifty-seven—don't all old people get backaches? But then she saw a million doctors and even started going for acupuncture. Seriously. Needles in her back, head, and God knows where else. And now they think it's her *pancreas*? For the first time, I wonder if something's really wrong. My stomach drops, like my own organs are sliding out.

At school, I don't mention the appointment to Shari or Hailee. During lunch at McDonald's, I keep it a secret from Tony and the guys from our band. It's not until I'm walking to class with Laura in the afternoon that I let on about Mom's doctor appointment. And it's only because Laura's playing her favorite game, 20 Questions—except with Laura it's more like 20,000 Questions.

"What's wrong?" she asks right away, her big blue eyes searching my face for clues. It's like she has a special radar for my misery. I guess best friends are weird like that—when something's wrong, they just know. After some prodding, I take a breath and finally confess.

"Um, my mom has a doctor appointment today."

"*Another* one?" she asks loudly, looking at me. "Which doctor?"

"Stomach."

"Why?"

"He thinks something might be wrong with her, um, pancreas."

"Her pancreas?" Laura sucks in her breath. "Maris, that's not good."

"I know," I admit, tearing up as I stare down at the hallway's puke green tiles. It feels so good—and so bad—to have someone voice the concern I've been carrying around all day.

She asks a million more questions—*Why do they think it's her pancreas? Why is she going to a stomach doctor and not a pancreas doctor?*—and I grow flustered because I don't know any of the answers. When the bell rings, for the first time ever I'm relieved we have to stop talking.

At dinner with Wilson that night, sitting stiffly at a fancy pizza place with white tablecloths and a tiny vase, I have the opposite problem: he barely says a word. But that's the thing about Wilson—he's practically mute. A few weeks ago at college, he went a whole day without saying a single word. When he told me about it later, I wasn't sure if he was proud or super depressed. Like me, he needs people to draw him out of his shell and make him talk. But sometimes I wonder if what Mom thinks is true, that maybe we're mismatched. Quiet meets quieter. Lonely meets loner. Actually, she thinks I'm too outgoing for him. She has no idea how contagious silence can be.

Is it weird that with the two closest people in my life—Laura and Wilson—one can't stop talking, and one can't start?

Sitting in the heavy silence of the pizza place, I work overtime to get words out of Wilson. *How's college life? What's your roommate like? Who's so-and-so?* I feel like Laura, firing off questions, and I'm relieved when Wilson asks about my family so that I have an opening to tell him about Mom's appointment. I think this could be the moment when the way I know he is deep down—gentle, caring, loving—finally comes to the surface. But I'm nervous, too. What if he's weird about it? What if he's *not* there for me?

Looking down at my plate, I mumble the words between cheesy bites of pizza—"doctor's appointment" (chew, chew) "something with her pancreas."

We've never had something really serious to discuss, other than whether we'd break up when he left for college (after a few weeks of being apart and miserable, we decided to stay together despite the thirteen-hour drive between us). But even that conversation seems small now compared to this, and I feel awkward, like I've brought something too heavy for us to hold. Slowly, I glance up at him.

"Wow," he says. His eyes widen behind his black plastic-framed glasses. "Is she OK?"

It's actually a big reaction for how shy he is. I release the breath I've been holding. Maybe this will be *the thing* that brings us closer together, *the thing* that solidifies our relationship forever.

"I dunno," I say shakily, looking at my watch and realizing it's nearly 8 p.m. "Her appointment was at four, so I guess I'll find out when I get home."

The drive home is torture. We take the quiet side streets we always take between Wilson's house and mine, passing through the suburban neighborhood in Long Island, New York, that I've lived in my whole life. It's pitch-black, but the streetlights shine on our charming elementary school and flicker across the dozens of houses and cars and lawns I know by heart. Finally, Wilson turns onto my street and my eyes instantly settle on home—halfway down the block, the brown house with the basketball hoop, that's mine.

Except it's all wrong. Immediately I know, because the driveway's empty, and they should have been home hours ago.

Where are they?

Where the *fuck* are they?

I crane my neck to look back out the rearview, then again out the front windshield. Any minute now. Right? Any minute now they'll pull up, and Dad will say something like, "Missy, the traffic, you wouldn't believe..." And Mom will say, "Oh Missy, you were worried? I'm sorry, doll. I'm fine. Everything's fine."

But it's not happening. The time is just ticking and ticking, the clock in Wilson's car blinking from 8:01 to 8:02, and still no sign of them.

I turn to Wilson, panicked, but it's like he forgot all about our conversation at the pizzeria. Sliding into our usual spot under the big oak tree, he turns off the motor just enough to keep the mix tape playing. Like it's just another make-out session. And all I can picture is my parents grief-stricken in some bleak doctor's office.

I bite my nails and stare out the car window at my house, anything I can do to show I'm freaking out. The questions in my head seem too juvenile to ask: "Where are they?" "Why aren't they home yet?" "What if something's really wrong?" *He's in college*, I remind myself. *Don't be a high school crybaby.*

Wilson cups his hands together and blows hot air inside them. The heat shut off in his beat-up Nissan Sentra, and it's instantly cold. He pulls my hands toward his mouth and does the same, his breath warm on my palms. He's trying, in his own way. Maybe I should try, too.

"It's so weird they're not home yet," I murmur finally.

Still warming my hands, Wilson's voice is a gravelly vibration on my fingertips: "Mmm."

It's his default reply. The one he uses when he's thinking, or uncomfortable, or not sure what to say. I should expect it, or at least be used to it by now. And yet that brief sound, that non-word word, makes me wish I'd said nothing at all. Then I could still hold onto his concern at the pizzeria instead of his silence now. It grows until it takes up more space in the car than us, even louder than the music playing from his stereo.

Slowly, I pull my hands away from him. If he kisses me, I'll cry. I can already feel the tears rising in my throat. And I don't cry in front of people. Not even my mom or Laura. If I need to cry, it's alone in my room with the door shut and my music blasting. That's it. In fact, that's where I'd like to be right now.

"I should go in," I say, reaching for the door handle.

"Wait," he says, touching my arm, his voice husky and soft.

I turn back toward him. Finally, he knows that I need him, and he'll comfort me.

"This is a really good song," he says, and turns up the volume. "Just listen."

I force myself to stay until the end of the song. Maybe out of politeness or wanting to seem cool or because the song is actually *really fucking good* or because he has this hold on me that I hate and love.

When it's over, I worry it's all my fault, that I've just been a weirdo all night. I tell him I liked the song. I give him a playful kiss on the cheek and close the car door. I trot up to my house in a way I hope looks cute and carefree. I hate that I still want him to like me. Love me. Whatever.

My hands shake as I fit the key into the lock, creeped out about coming home to a dark house and waiting for my parents by myself. But I quickly realize that my older brother, Jordan, is *definitely* home. As usual, his door is shut, but that does nothing to drown out the noise: Rusted Root blasting so loud it's like they're playing live in my brother's room. Like Wilson, he's home from college on winter break, and the song's lyrics speak to his joy at being reunited with his family: "Send me on my way…"

"Hi…" I call up the stairs, even though I know he can't hear me.

In the movie version, the big brother would comfort the little sister until the parents got home. After all, Mom told him about the appointment, too. But that would involve him actually acknowledging that I exist. He must care a little because he pauses the music to yell through the door, "They called to say they'll be late," before hitting "play" again.

Trudging upstairs to my bedroom, I continue to watch for my parents' car from the big picture window that faces the driveway. I splay my elbows on the windowsill and rest a cheek on my arm. Tears leak out onto my sleeve. It's my mom and not my mom. It's Wilson and not Wilson. It's leaving for college in the fall and not even knowing where I'm going. It's everything. I used to daydream about the future, as if it were rolled out before me like a red carpet, but now it just feels like one big, looming question mark. *Where will I go to college? What will I be? Who will I marry?* I wish I could know all the answers, but Mom says life wouldn't be nearly as fun that way.

Headlights curve around the corner, and my head jerks up.

White minivan. Not them.

The street is still until another set of headlights leer toward my house. It's them, I can tell. The purr of the motor, the slow speed Dad crawls to when he's within a block or two of our house, the way Dad uses his blinker even though we live on a dead-end street that's pretty much desolate. They park, but no one gets out for a while. My heart is pounding. Finally, Dad slowly emerges and stretches, peering up at the night sky. Mom seems to take more time than usual in the passenger seat, stuffing items into her purse and checking her reflection in the vanity mirror. Is she wiping away tears or just excess eyeliner? It's too dark to tell.

I race downstairs toward the front door, but freeze on the last step. I feel like I'm in a movie: where should I stand when they deliver the news? I debate running back to my room and pretending to do homework, but it's too late. Keys scrape into the lock, and there they are.

Still perched on the last step, reluctant to meet them all the way, I lean forward and peer out at them.

"Hi, Miss," Mom says softly. Her big smile appears on autopilot, then retracts to a worried line. My heart lifts then sinks alongside it.

"Hiii…" I say. It comes out cautious and hollow. So many questions—How are you? Where have you been? Why did it take so long? And, oh yeah, *what the hell is going on?*—but I can't bring myself to ask. I want to know and don't want to know. I should have stayed in my room.

Dad holds out a hanger as Mom removes her coat, and then busies himself putting it into the closet. He hasn't said a word. Mom's taking tissues from her purse and stuffing them into the pockets of her jeans. My parents are ten years older than my friends' parents—they met later in life, and Mom didn't have me until she was thirty-nine—but tonight they *look* old.

Everything's moving in slow motion, and I can't take it anymore.

"What's wrong?" I blurt out.

Mom and Dad exchange a look.

"We should get Jordan…" Mom says pointedly to Dad, clearly wanting him to endure the task of trying to corral my brother. Dad sighs and shuts the closet door, then turns toward the staircase.

"Jordan!" Dad yells up from the foot of the stairs, Mom beside him, me a foot away still perched on the stairs.

I shoot Dad a dirty look and rub the ear he yelled in. He raises his bushy eyebrows helplessly—as if to ask, *What do you want from me, Missy?*—then returns to glaring past me upstairs. I instantly regret my position in the crossfire, yet feel unable to move.

"Jordan!" Dad yells again, jaw clenched, hand gripping the banister.

Still no response. I roll my eyes. Jordan's a junior in college, but trying to summon him is just as annoying as it was in high school.

"JORDAN!" Dad hollers, a deep roar that makes me jump. When he gets angry, it's so different from his quiet and patient demeanor that it's downright frightening.

The bedroom door swings open wildly, and Jordan lunges forward. A too-tight Abercrombie T-shirt pulls across his too-muscular chest. My friends think he's hot, with his dark eyes and chiseled face, but they don't know what a jerk he can be. I flinch backward a bit.

"WHAT?" Jordan yells down at us.

"I called you three times!" Dad scowls. "Come downstairs."

"What do you want? I'm busy!" He's definitely *not* busy, and just nervous like I am. That's why he's being such an asshole. But still, we have to play his game.

"Just come downstairs," Dad says, trying his calm middle-school guidance counselor voice. It probably works on his students, but Jordan is a different species.

"Come downstairs," my brother mimics in a high-pitched voice. "I'm right here—talk."

Dad, surrendering both palms, shoots an exasperated look at Mom.

"Jor, can you just come down for a minute?" Mom asks gently, squeezing past Dad and looking up at my brother.

Jordan's brooding, but no longer refusing. Mom's harder to read. She looks like a slumped version of herself. Eyes small and meek without this morning's makeup. Wispy hair flat from running her fingers through it too many times. Striped sweater bunched up in the back instead of smoothed over her jeans. Normally I can tell exactly how she's feeling. Just one look, and I know. But when she glances over at me, her gaze is shallow. Tiny ripples where an ocean used to be.

"Please, Jor?" Mom says to Jordan, and there's only kindness in her voice, her eyes. "It's been a long day."

She has a way with him, always has.

"Fine," Jordan huffs.

It's such a feat to get everyone downstairs, and yet when we reach the den, everyone stands around awkwardly. A recliner and an L-shaped couch stare at us. It's a living room rarely lived in, and no one knows where to sit. We have assigned seats at the kitchen table on the opposite side of the room, and we all look over there as if searching for clues. But it's not like we ever talk there. We're the only family I know that watches *Seinfeld* reruns during dinner, not because Jordan and I beg for it but because our parents want to.

Finally, Dad sits on the edge of the recliner. Mom follows his lead, curling up on the end of the couch closest to him. Jordan plunges himself into the cushy corner of the L, arms crossed. I stake out the far end of the couch and hug my knees to my chest.

This feels weird. We never all sit on the couch, a taupe sectional with leopard print throw pillows that's more catalog-worthy than comfortable. Being busy is our thing. Mom and Dad teach forty minutes away in Queens, my brother lives four hours away at college, and I bounce between band practice, yearbook committee, and hanging out with my friends. When we all finally come home after a long day, we usually separate; a chance to catch our breath after being surrounded by people all day.

Now, with all of us seated together, it feels like we're pretending to be some kind of picture-perfect family. I look suspiciously at the vase on the mantelpiece and imagine a camera nestled inside, secretly taping us. I think of Lifetime movies and Barbara Walters interviews and other, more proper families who might be better prepared to do this. Families accustomed to sitting together on couches.

Everyone shifts awkwardly. Mom takes a deep breath. I can't handle it. Silence had filled my day. Silence from Wilson. Silence from my brother. Silence from my parents. I crave words.

Speak!

SPEAK!!!

She says words, but they're not true. Something about the pancreas…and tumors…and maybe it's in the liver, but the doctors don't know…biopsy…tests.

I keep thinking this isn't real. It can't be real. I look around at my mom tearing up, my dad looking down, my brother staring in disbelief. Self-consciously, I wonder what I look like. Do I look the way characters in movies look when they get news like this? No, I decide. They're always prettier than I am, as if their beauty can balance their bad luck. Girls like me, families like mine—this isn't how our story is supposed to go.

I'm confused, too, because in movies, this is the way it happens: the mom sits the family down and starts with something like "This is hard to say," or "I don't know how to tell you this." And then she says: "I have cancer."

But Mom's not saying that. I measure her speech against the ones in the movies and decide Mom *doesn't* have cancer. Instead, I hold onto the one piece that sounds hopeful: the doctors won't know for sure what's going on until the biopsy results come back.

Exhaling a breath I didn't know I'd been holding, I reassure myself that we'll soon discover this has all been a mistake. I picture myself at lunch with Tony and the guys next week, telling them the crazy story of Mom's misdiagnosis. "I was terrified," I'll confess, as Tony puts a comforting arm around me.

I'm feeling a little better until I realize Mom's still talking, and that she's saved the worst for last.

"Two months to live," Mom says, and she begins to cry. Not the way a woman weeps, not the way she cries when we get into fights, but high-pitched hiccups. She rubs her tiny hazel eyes like a child.

Two months to live. Two months to live. That's all I hear, over and over again. But I can't make sense of it. It feels like all of it is happening around me, but can't possibly be happening to me. I keep waiting for the thing that makes it untrue. A "just kidding," or "but don't worry because," or that moment when I wake up from this horrible dream. I blink and blink, but each time I open my eyes all I see is Mom crying.

I know I should comfort my mom, but I can't. I picture the role of the good daughter—rushing over and embracing her, crying by her side—but I don't move. Her hiccup tears keep coming, and I'm horrified and repelled by them. When Dad reaches out to her, holding her hand and shushing her, I'm relieved to be off the hook. Especially since my thoughts are relentless, rushing past like a nightmarish daydream.

I think of prom. I imagine a green lawn and jewel-toned dresses and all the mothers taking pictures. Except mine. June is five months away—my mom will be dead.

I think of graduation. I'm in a cap and gown looking out into the bleachers at a sea of parents, but I can't find her. June is five months away—my mom will be dead.

I think of college. All the schools I'd applied to were four or five hours away. How can I leave home and desert my family?

Our taupe sectional seems to divide into islands, and I'm left alone, clutching a leopard-print throw pillow like a life jacket.

Mom fishes a crumpled pink Kleenex out of her pocket, blows her nose loudly, and somehow tries to smile at me. I'm horrified when I hear what comes out of my mouth: a giggle. It's my normal reflex, but it's so wrong that I clutch my hand over my mouth and begin to cry. Another giggle escapes, then a sob. And another. I never cry in front of them, and I don't know what's more humiliating: the inappropriateness of the giggles or the vulnerability of the sobs.

"Poor Missy, you don't know how to feel," Mom soothes, coming to sit beside me. "I'm sorry. I'm so sorry, doll."

She rubs my back and reaches out to Jordan, but he doesn't move. My parents ask if he's all right, offer that he can take the semester off, but he only responds with a small twitch of his head.

"I've had such a good life, and I love you all so much," Mom says through tears. "You'll be OK. Daddy will take care of you."

Dad's been silent this whole time, just running his thumb and forefinger over his eyebrows again and again. At the mention of his name, he pauses to regard us with bloodshot green eyes. Sure, he goes grocery shopping and pays the bills, but the idea of him taking care of us is unfathomable. We all know it's Mom who holds us together.

That's when I realize. The thing I'd been dreading—that Mom could be sick—seems innocent and naïve now. This isn't a conversation about how to deal with Mom's illness. This is a conversation about what we'll do after Mom is dead.

Marisa / **Sally**

I always thought I would die in a car crash. I would be driving on a dark highway and headlights would come right at me. Suddenly, a Mack truck would zoom right into my car. And I would be dead.

That speeding ticket in my twenties really did a number on me.

Seriously, one measly ticket on I-95, and—bam!—your life can change. No accident, no injuries, but that highway patrol officer scared the crap out of me. I haven't hit the gas on a highway ever since, leaving all the long-distance drives to Bill. I can't even take Missy to the mall.

Trucks are not my fate, it turns out, but the news of my end came just as suddenly. It was January 13, and I thought I had many more years of my life to enjoy. Cancer disagreed. But I'm not ready to go.

———

I could lie here like this with Missy forever. Rhythmically stroking her back, feeling the calm wash over her and me. We are ageless in this moment. She is one, two, ten, seventeen, all of them combined. She is my quickly—too quickly—growing-up daughter, and I treasure the moments when she still needs her mommy.

Missy won't say that we're best friends, but I know we are. She just hasn't figured it out yet, I realize, as I tuck my brown blanket around her. Sometimes it's a slow transition; sometimes it's an "aha" moment. With my mom, it was the latter. A breast cancer diagnosis will do that. Especially when you're fourteen and terrified of losing your mother.

Missy shifts her weight, and I sadden at the thought of her leaving. Not only now, but for college in the fall. She rolls out of bed and sheepishly waves goodnight, as if embarrassed by her childlike pose of lying beside me—but when I reach out my arms for a hug, she gives in. My girl.

I have trouble sleeping, and the next morning my voice shakes as I tell Missy we have yet another doctor's appointment after work. I can't tell if she's nervous or if she just thinks her mom is a hypochondriac. But the word "pancreas" seems to frighten us both, so foreign and unknown.

After a busy day at work—Bill as a middle school guidance counselor, me as an elementary school special ed teacher, with schools just a few minutes apart from each other in Queens—Bill picks me up and drives us to the doctor. We trade stories about our days, and I regale him with my usual wild tales about my students. Like today, when one of my favorite students, Alfred, interrupted me mid-lesson to announce his new nickname for me: "Little Miss Bardach." Boy, did the class laugh at that. Most of them have been kept back so many times that even though they're only in elementary school, they tower over me. Bill, who always teases me for being short—even though I'm five-foot-and-a-half-inch, thankyouverymuch—gets a good chuckle out of this one. He reaches over to turn up the volume on the radio, recognizing some '80s song that he hums along to in his playful way.

But Bill quickly turns serious as we navigate to a radiology center we've never been to before. Dr. Zinberg, my stomach doctor, said we must go right away for a sonogram of my abdomen, and the only appointment we could get quickly enough is in Howard Beach,

Queens—far from our schools and our house in Long Island. Bill has a great sense of direction, but always gets anxious when we have to drive somewhere new. To be honest, I think the doctor's urgency has us both on edge. The radiologist will send the sonogram to Dr. Zinberg immediately, and then we have to drive directly to his office for the results. It's a bit nerve-racking, to say the least.

I expect the radiology center to be a big, ominous building, and I'm surprised when Bill parallel parks beside a strip mall. Situated between Platinum Discount Deals and 50% Off Cards & Gifts, a flimsy sign that flaps in the wind reads South Shore Radiology. "I better not end up with a Junior Mint in my stomach," I quip to Bill, referencing one of our favorite *Seinfeld* episodes about a botched surgery. But secretly I pray to God that these people know what they're doing.

God must have listened because the receptionist is a hoot—a bawdy broad with a booming laugh who calls me "Sugar" when she hands me a stack of paperwork to fill out. She immediately puts me at ease. Laughing along with her, I can't help but relax. That is, until they call my name, and it's time for me to go in.

Leaving Bill in the waiting room, the receptionist whisks me away to a small exam room with a "Diseases of the Digestive System" poster featured prominently on the wall. I don't get doctor art. Do they really expect me to study the sausage-like intestines and diagnose myself? I change into a coarse blue robe—the one that's eighteen sizes too big and flatters no one. After what feels like an eternity, the radiologist enters. She's young and pretty, Indian with long brown hair and big brown eyes. The kind of beautiful ease I'd like to come back with in my next life. In a measured voice, she asks me to open my robe so that she can perform the ultrasound. Globs of cold petroleum jelly on my belly make me flinch, giving me déjà vu of my pregnancies. "This was a lot more fun twenty years ago when there was a baby inside," I joke. The radiologist smiles briefly, then returns to her serious concentration. Back then, the fear was looking inside and finding nothing. Now the fear is finding something.

I try to read the expression of the radiologist, but they must practice these poker faces in medical school. I imagine a whole class about it, the professor lecturing: "Now class, resume the non-expression. Squint slightly—no, I didn't say furrow your brows. That implies worry. It's more of a snobbish, intellectual squint."

It's been a long day, and since she's not up for chatting and I'm leaning back anyway, I close my eyes. I picture Bill in the waiting room, anxiously checking the clock. I imagine Jordan holed up in his bedroom, music blasting, staring at the ceiling deep in thought. I think of Missy out to dinner with Wilson, looking pretty with her freshly washed curls, and wonder if she's told him that I'm here. I wish I could tell them not to worry, but I'm worried, too.

The sonogram is fairly quick, but by the time Bill and I drive in heavy rush-hour traffic from Queens to Dr. Zinberg's office in Long Island, a few towns away from where we live, it's already dark outside. Normally I know the receptionists at the doctors we go to regularly, and enjoy chatting about our days or asking after their children, but not at Dr. Zinberg's office. The doctors and staff are all Orthodox Jewish, and the glass partition separating the staff from the patients tells you exactly how much they want to interact. The funny thing is I grew up Orthodox Jewish, but quickly rejected it once I was out on my own (preferring the more lax Reform Judaism), and once you remove yourself from the clan, it's as if you were never in it.

I jot down my name on the sign-in sheet, and Bill and I relax into the dingy-yet-familiar waiting room chairs. We all have bad stomachs on my side of the family, and I've been coming here for years. But this time, the word *pancreas* keeps zipping into my brain. I try to shut it out, along with the other scary words slipping in. You can't have my family history and *not* have the C-word in your head— but I've lived with that fear my whole life, so in some ways, this is nothing new. I reassure myself that the problem is likely minor. Maybe even miniscule. And you know what, the doctor will tell us what to do, and we'll do it, I decide. That's that. Bill gives my shoulder a comforting squeeze.

I leaf through the magazine selection on the table beside me and have become absorbed in an article on "America's Top Colleges" when a nurse calls my name. Quickly, she leads us through a maze of sterile offices and procedure rooms until she finally stops at a small exam room. Bill slumps into a straight-back chair. I sit on the exam table, feeling like a little girl as the paper crinkles beneath me and my boots thud against the metal base. I'm still gripping the magazine but no longer able to concentrate, since I'm sure the doctor will be in any minute.

But the minutes tick by until it's been twenty minutes, forty minutes. We sit up straight each time we hear footsteps in the corridor, certain the doctor is coming in to see me. But each time we hear him open a different door and greet a different patient. Our bodies go slack with a mix of disappointment and relief. From my parents' bouts with cancer, I know that once you know the news, you can't un-know it.

Bill and I talk quietly, nervously, constantly looking at the door. It's hard to talk about anything other than the wait. We're too distracted to even talk about little things, like what we'll make for dinner tonight or what we'll do this weekend. Normal life seems to disappear within these beige walls.

"What the hell is taking so long?" Bill demands, pacing the small room, always so protective of me. We've never had to wait this long before, and it feels like a bad omen.

When Bill can't take it any longer, he storms to the reception desk to ask how much longer it will be. The women are curt, as usual, giving robotic replies that the doctor will be in any minute. By the third time he checks in, they busy themselves with filing and phone calls, no longer even willing to give him the time of day. It's business as usual with this oh-so-friendly staff.

Bill comes back to the room more agitated than before, which only makes me more anxious, too. We hear doors open and patients leave, so why does the doctor keep skipping us? It's late in the day, and we've been waiting for over an hour, and it feels like they're getting rid of everyone else before coming to talk to me.

I grow more and more anxious, which makes my stomach upset, and I spend much of the time treading a path between the exam room and the bathroom down the hall. It's always been my body's reaction to stress, from throwing up my cereal and milk before school as a little girl to running to the bathroom at my favorite deli after Bill announced he wanted to buy our house. However, the irony of having an upset stomach because of the wait at the stomach doctor's office is not lost on me. I make a crack about it to Bill, and he forces a laugh, but then returns to worriedly rubbing his eyebrows.

Finally, after what feels like two hours, there's a brusque knock on the door, and Dr. Zinberg strides in. He's typically so friendly, but this time he rushes the hellos and how are yous. I remind myself it's late in the day, people want to get home—us included. Jordan and Missy must be worried sick.

I try to catch Bill's eye, but he's looking at the doctor. Dr. Zinberg is the youngest, yet the most personable, of the three doctors in the practice. That's why I've always seen him. But today he seems cold and uncomfortable. He fidgets with his maroon tie, which is flecked with tiny navy diamonds, as he places a sonogram image on the light board.

"I'm sorry to have to tell you this, but it's probably a malignant tumor in the pancreas," Dr. Zinberg says, pointing at a white splotch. "With possible spots on the liver, as well."

Stunned, I sit dumbfounded while the doctor ticks off statistics about pancreatic cancer. I ask question after question, trying to get a hopeful response. After all, I've gone to his office whenever I've had stomach trouble for the past—oh, who knows?—probably fifteen years. Prescriptions, diet changes, exercise—I'll do anything. Certainly he'll have a solution.

"Patient survival rate is minimal," he says.

When I press him, he hesitates, then says it's typically a matter of months—maybe two, maybe six, it's hard to tell.

"I could die in two months?" I repeat in disbelief.

Dr. Zinberg doesn't correct me.

Bill and I glare at him. We can't bear to face each other.

When I argue it was just a backache, Dr. Zinberg explains that the other doctors misdiagnosed me. My pain wasn't muscle spasms or anything acupuncture would help cure. Back pain is actually one of the warning signs of pancreatic cancer, he says. That's why it's so hard to catch early—because back pain is so common among older adults.

"I'm going to die. I don't believe it. How am I going to tell my kids? What do I tell them?" I repeat this over and over again, barely recognizing my voice, which sounds faraway and robotic.

Dr. Zinberg doesn't mention chemotherapy, doesn't refer me to another doctor or specialist, doesn't say anything hopeful at all. Finally, he speaks.

"Why don't you wait until after the biopsy of the pancreas? We'll know more then."

"It's Missy's high school graduation," I whisper, as if God could postpone this awful news until after I see her in her cap and gown.

We sit for a few minutes longer, but it becomes clear there's nothing left to say. Dr. Zinberg walks us toward the reception area. I glare at the back of his wrinkled Oxford shirt, my hands shaking with anger as I grip the leather strap of my purse. How could he tell us this and be so unfeeling, so final? I catch a glimpse of him as we part ways, and he looks almost as miserable as we must. I soften, realizing he's used to performing colonoscopies and other routine procedures. Of course he doesn't have a bedside manner; this is not a usual part of his day. I give his hand a squeeze.

Bill and I numbly put on our winter coats and walk huddled together to the car. We drive home in silence, which we never do, unless I'm right in the middle of a good book, and even then Bill always has the radio on. For once, I can't think of anything to say. There's nothing I can say to make this better, or to make it go away.

A sob is clenched in my throat as one thought keeps nagging me: my work here is not *done*. Getting married and having children happened so late for me—marriage at thirty-four, kids at thirty-six and thirty-nine. For years before I met Bill I thought I was destined to be a spinster: the funny single gal who kept choosing the wrong men. Falling in love with Bill and having a family changed everything for me. But the best part of my life feels like it's just begun—and I still have so much more to do. I'm supposed to help Missy transition to college. I need to make sure Jordan graduates from college and adjusts to adulthood. And Bill and I have big plans to retire from our teaching jobs and travel the world: Australia, Alaska, maybe even back to beautiful Hawaii. The next phase of our lives is about to open up. Now it will just end? It seems too cruel.

Suddenly, Bill pulls over to the side of the road.

"Billy!" I scream, startled.

He sobs loudly and clutches me. I clutch him back, sobbing into his scratchy coat.

How can this be us? How can this be the end of my life, the end of our life together? I don't want to go. *Please, please, please God, don't make me go.*

Through my sobs, I can't stop apologizing to Bill: "I'm sorry. I'm so, so sorry." I feel so guilty, so angry with my body. How could I leave him with our two children who still have so much growing to do, who still need us so much? He's a wonderful father, but still, we were supposed to do this together, always.

We stay in our embrace for what feels like an eternity. We're only blocks away from our house, but it feels like we're in another world. I think of all the times we've been in this part of the neighborhood to do everyday things, like buy a gallon of milk or pick up the dry cleaning. The mundane tasks that make up our lives. Now all I want is a million chances to do them again and again. To just be here.

I blow my nose loudly and try to pull myself together, to be strong for my husband.

"Billy, do you want me to drive the rest of the way?" I ask him. I hate driving at night, but tonight I almost feel like I could do anything. I imagine a marketing campaign for the DMV: Get cancer—and get over your fear of driving! I can be the spokeswoman...

"No, I can do it." Bill wipes his eyes and blows his nose loudly into a handkerchief. In twenty-two years of marriage I've never seen him so upset. I feel like I'm watching an actor in a movie; surely this can't be my calm, steady husband stifling sobs as he starts the car.

Truth be told, I'm relieved he'll drive. Whenever I get behind the wheel, Bill sounds like a Driver's Ed instructor. Patiently, he offers gentle reminders like, "Check your blind spot," and when the sun shines after a storm, "You probably don't need your windshield wipers anymore, honey." But two weeks ago he lost his patience and barked, "Sal! You're blind! You need to get your eyes checked!" as he glared back apologetically at the stop sign I had just run.

"What are we going to tell the kids?" he asks now, looking over at me.

Bill's meaty palm grips the shift lever. The car is still in park, and I know he can't continue driving until we decide. This goddamn awful decision about when to break our children's hearts.

"I don't know. Dr. Zinberg said we should wait until after the biopsy. Maybe he's right."

"We can't keep this from them—we're too emotional," he says. His years of being a middle-school guidance counselor often give him so much wisdom as a parent.

I agree with him, but as he pulls back onto the road, I dread returning home. Jordan and Missy are still so young, just twenty and seventeen. Of course, they aren't babies anymore. Children much younger had been given news like this, I'm sure. But still, they're *my* babies. Jordan still has a year and a half left at college in Rhode Island. And Missy's still in high school. She just finished applying to five colleges; Binghamton and Penn State have already accepted her. Will my news derail all their plans?

We stay in the driveway for a few moments to compose ourselves in the car, but we know we're only fooling ourselves. I feel like crying as soon as we open the door. Just the thought of telling our children tears me apart inside. *Compose yourself*, I scold myself. *Keep your act together for your kids.*

I avoid Missy's questioning gaze, for fear of breaking down, and Bill asks Jordan to come downstairs so we can all sit on our sofa in the family room. Jordan needs some extra prodding, but eventually he joins us. Half the room is a dining room, which is where we spend most of our time together, eating dinner and watching *Seinfeld* reruns. It's a lovely room with pegged wood floors, a red brick fireplace, and sunny skylights. Now, it's dark and the room feels eerie, as if I've died already and only my spirit is sitting here.

"I think this is the first time we've *ever* sat on the couch together," my husband comments. His corny jokes always make our kids laugh. This time, I laugh too, relieved that, for a second, things feel normal.

I look at Bill, even though I know I'll be the one to tell them. His eyes are sad but encouraging. It's the little check-in I need so that I can be brave for our children.

"The doctor…" I start, then stop. How do I say this without scaring them to death? I take a deep breath. "The doctor found a… uh, spot. On my pancreas."

I can tell they're confused. A spot? But all the other words sound terrifying. Although my being vague is probably just as scary.

"A spot meaning, um, a tumor. Probably a malignant tumor…" Do they know the difference between malignant and benign? "… which is, um, the bad kind."

I'm careful not to say "cancer," but then realize how silly it is to protect them from that, given what I have to tell them next. So I just say it all.

"So, um, the doctor thinks it's probably pancreatic cancer."

The words hang in the air. I struggle to fill the silence.

"He says that survival rates aren't very good." My voice is getting thin and shaky. I look at Bill again, but he's gazing down at the carpet. "And that...that I might have only two months to live."

Shock registers on their faces. They don't say anything. I don't think they can speak. Desperate to fill the silence, I try to repeat all the information Dr. Zinberg told me. But everything I say sounds hopeless.

"I'm sorry," I apologize again and again, desperate for them to know my misery over hurting them, over leaving them. "I didn't want to put a hole in your hearts."

Missy laughs and cries at the same time. I sit beside her, pull her toward me, and rub her back. Jordan just sits there frozen, his face and hands not moving, in total shock. At one point, I tell him he can take the semester off if he wants to. He doesn't respond; I'm not even sure if he heard me. He just sits glued to the sectional. Fear and anger cover his face. Disbelief covers Missy's.

"I've had a wonderful life with your Daddy," I say, wanting them to see the good. "I'm so extremely lucky and proud to have two such terrific children. You always bring me a great deal of joy—" Tears trap the rest of my words.

How wonderful my children are. I think of Jordan sitting at the piano after dinner, playing for us the new masterpiece he has composed. "Listen!" he yells, getting mad if we talk over the music. And Missy, bringing home a 93 on an English paper and griping about the seven points that were taken off "for no reason," worrying about getting into Cornell and wondering what major will make her happiest. I saw her play drums in an all-male band last month. Bill and I whooped and hollered from the audience. We were so proud. Bill will have to go see her alone now.

The phone interrupts my thoughts, and our conversation.

We all look at Missy, since calls are usually for her. She gets up slowly and picks up the phone in the kitchen. "Laura? Can I call you back…?" She hangs up and walks tentatively back to the couch. I've moved back next to Bill and I hope she'll come sit near me, hug me, but she goes back to the far end of the couch where she was sitting before. I've broken her heart.

Desperate, I reach for anything the doctor told us that was hopeful. Finally, I repeat what the doctor said: nothing will be definite until we get back results from the biopsy. Jordan doesn't move; Missy looks relieved. I worry that I've given her false hope, but it *is* what the doctor said. Who knows what's right or wrong at this point. I'm pretending I know how to do this, but I'm just as lost as they are.

It's quiet in the living room the same way it was in the doctor's office. There's so much to say and yet nothing left to say—at least not right now. Still, no one moves, each of us alone in our grief. I can't stand to see my family so broken. I have to make this better, I have to do something, anything. I glance at the clock and realize my favorite show is on. Maybe I'm pretending nothing's wrong, but right now I'm craving anything that makes things feel normal.

"*Seinfeld's* on!" I say, too loudly, jumping up from the couch.

Bill must be wanting a break from this awful reality, too, because he quickly finds the remote and flips to the show. It's an episode I've seen a million times, but I laugh in a way I hope sounds like my real laugh, begging my family to join in.

"You gotta keep laughing, right?" I say out loud to no one in particular.

Our family has always had a good sense of humor, and as strange as it feels to laugh, I know we will need it to get through this terrible time.

I move to my chair at the head of the kitchen table so I can watch the show while I eat some grapes that Bill washed and set out for me. Jordan moves to the recliner. Bill rinses cereal bowls left in the sink from breakfast. Missy stands and watches for a few minutes, then backs up slowly and goes upstairs to her room, probably to call Laura. I wonder what best friends say in situations like these.

And now, with my news today, I worry I'm out of the running. What daughter wants to be best friends with someone who's dying?

The next day, I have to call some of my best friends, too. I dial my very dear friend, Rona, whose father suffered from cancer. She tells me about Dr. Bruckner, a specialist in pancreatic cancer who's rumored to have kept patients alive for ten years. It isn't great—but it's better than two months. I book an appointment, daydreaming about a future that, although cut short, now, by contrast, feels long.

Ten more years with my husband.

Ten more years to see my son turn thirty. A man, imagine that.

Ten more years to see my daughter turn twenty-seven—and a chance to fight for her friendship.

CHAPTER 2
Reactions

Marisa / Sally

"Marisa, what's wrong with your mother's pancreas?" Laura's voice trembles over the phone. No *hi* or *what's up*. Have I already been moved to this "other" category where normal talk is forbidden? She's my best friend in the world, yet I have an overwhelming urge to hang up.

"I dunno," I mumble, trying to sound casual, to do anything to calm that pleading voice on the other end. "They think there might be a tumor—but they won't know until after they take a biopsy."

"Caaancer?" she breathes. "Oh, Marisa…" I imagine her big blue eyes welling up with tears. God, she can be so overdramatic. The doctor didn't say anything was definite yet. They haven't even done the biopsy. Irritated, I say, "Well, I guess I should go spend time with her." I stay in my room the rest of the night.

My only other call that night is to Wilson. Like me, he's shocked into silence, but I have no sympathy. He's my boyfriend. I want him to get me so intimately that he knows exactly how I feel and exactly what to say. "He's not a mind reader, Missy," Mom likes to tease me.

But why the hell not? Tonight he responds in mumbles and murmurs until finally I explode, "Don't you even care?" He bursts back, "She's my friend, too!" His reaction surprises me: he does care—and he's more attached to her than I'd realized. My mom just has this effect on people. But how can he compare his friendship with my mom to her being *my mom*? I hang up feeling like he doesn't get it at all.

I sit on my bed and try to do AP English homework, but it's useless. Each sentence of *The Awakening* ends with me staring off into space or gazing up at my bulletin board. I'd spent the past few weeks on my bedroom floor hunched over the board, curating a cluttered collage of concert ticket stubs and *Seventeen* magazine cutouts and dozens of photos: my Sweet Sixteen at NYC's South Street Seaport, a summer trip with my cousins to L.A., playing drums with the guys at band practice. The girl with the curls is smiling in every picture, and I resent her already. Her happiness. Her innocence. How clueless she is. The board I've worked on so intensely for weeks now taunts me, like a time capsule of the smiling girl I was before all this, the girl I'll never be again. And if I'm not the smiling girl, who will I become?

Too exhausted to finish my homework or return Tony or Shari's calls, or even say goodnight to my parents, I turn off my light and bury myself under my pastel comforter. Weezer's "Butterfly," their saddest ballad, fills the room, and I loop the song so it repeats. But in the brief silence between loops, Mom's words rush back to me, and I beg the song to start again to drown out her words and my sobs.

"Miss?" I hear my mom call from her bedroom upstairs. Quickly, I shut off my stereo and wipe my face on the comforter before bur-rowing beneath it. A moment later my door creaks open as she peeks into the dark room. "Miss? You asleep already?" Her voice sounds raspy from sobbing, and I can't bear to face her. I feign sleep until she leaves, and soon I even trick myself, crashing into a comatose slumber.

Somehow I go to school the next day. It's a Friday. Mom says I can stay home, but I don't want to. My body is on autopilot, and there's something soothing about my usual routine. I pull on jeans and a hoodie, but in the full-length mirror, scared eyes stare back at me. Will people know just by looking at me? Will they know my life just changed overnight? I try my best to conceal it. I paint my face with foundation. Draw lines of brown eyeliner. Scrunch gel into my dark curls. Grab my bag and car keys. Leave.

First period is AP Calculus. I walk in ten minutes late, head hung low, avoiding eye contact with my teacher and classmates. Since I'm late to school almost every day, no one even notices anything is wrong. It's the opposite of that time Jenny burst into tears in class, confessing that her father had a heart attack the night before. Part of me longs to be the girl whose emotions explode so easily. It seems so freeing. But that's not me. My feelings are always stuck just under the surface, a bubbling volcano apparent only to me. Looking around the classroom, I realize how easy it will be to hide the news about my mom forever, which makes me feel both safe and scared.

I take out my notebook, but can't follow Mr. MacMullen's lesson. What if I can't focus in class ever again? What if I can't graduate high school? Then I remember I've never understood derivatives. I copy down the day's notes and hope he doesn't call on me. Laura tries to catch my eye, but her concern just leaves me feeling prickly. I stare at the blackboard and try to make my gaze stoic, unreadable.

"Are you going to tell Shari?" Laura hounds me at my locker as I exchange books after class.

"No," I say sharply. I look around to see if anyone overheard her. "Don't say anything to anyone. Not until after the biopsy."

That's when I'll tell people, I decide—once the doctors realize they're wrong and it's only arthritis or something stupid like that. Laura leaves for her next class, promising to call me later. "Or maybe don't," I want to say, but hold my tongue. I know I'm not really being fair to her, and that I need her.

I linger at my locker. Two girls walk arm in arm down the hall, snapping gum and screaming dramatically about something ridiculous. The popular kids huddle in the main lobby as if it's a velvet-roped VIP section, making weekend plans and gossiping until the bell rings. They seem so normal; their concerns so trivial. Was it only yesterday I was one of them?

Seventeen was supposed to be my perfect age. I'd been waiting to reach it since I subscribed to *Seventeen* (at age thirteen, of course). When I was younger, I'd sketch myself at seventeen: tall, skinny, bigger boobs, sexy curls falling down my back, and bell-bottom jeans. OK, so in reality I'm five-foot-two and an A cup. But while I might be on the outskirts of the popular crowd, I've found my place. I have a group of best friends, a boyfriend, a band. On a good hair day and with the right outfit, I even feel pretty. It's my senior year, the time when everything in my life is supposed to happen. Now, with my mom, it all feels different. *I* feel different. But inside I'm still aching to be…I don't know who. I guess whoever it is I was becoming.

That afternoon in Chemistry class, Shari asks why I didn't call her back the night before. "I fell asleep early," I say, which is the truth, sort of. "Lucky. I had to wake up early to walk Romeo this morning," she complains about her beagle, who humps me every time I go to her house, usually in front of our cute guy friends. Later, in Band, I space out and miss a big drum roll. The conductor raises his arms, and Hailee playfully scolds me for losing my place. "I'm just tired," I say. "Me, too," she yawns. The lies come easily, and as I look around at the students packing up their flutes and trombones, I wonder how many others have secret lives like mine.

Cancer has killed some of my friends' parents already. In middle school, Colby's dad died of cancer, and then so did Morgan's mom. I paid a shiva call to Morgan, the first one I ever went to for a friend alone, without my parents. She was wearing a black dress. I wondered when she'd bought it, then quickly forgot once we all started playing Monopoly in her bedroom. That night, when my mom came into my room, I was extra quiet. "Morgan doesn't have a mom to tuck her in anymore," I said finally. She hugged me tight and held me for a while. It didn't matter that I was thirteen and too old to be tucked in.

I felt my friends' losses deeply. But I'm different than most people in my town. When you grow up in Long Island, even death turns into gossip. I know if I tell Shari or Hailee about my mom they'll tell others, and the others will tell more others, and pretty soon the whole school will be staring at me as I walk through the halls. Judging me, waiting for me to break down, shaking their heads and whispering to one another. I know everyone I *don't* want to know at my high school will approach me. All the rich bitches of the world who can never get enough gossip to clamp their teeth around. To them, I'd be just another chew toy.

Over the weekend at my house, grief takes over. My mom retires to her bedroom, taking breaks from her Danielle Steel novel to call relatives and friends and deliver the news. Her openness appalls me. Nearly hysterical, I make her promise she won't tell anyone who could leak it to someone at my school. She hesitates, citing the value of supportive friends, but agrees when she sees how shaken I am. My dad brings her Lemon Soother tea and clementines, her favorite. My brother, who usually holes himself in his room, makes hourly trips upstairs to check on her until he leaves to go back to college on Sunday. After so many years of him being a self-centered jerk who never wanted to spend time with us, I can't believe how much he's sucking up. But she falls for it. As he drives away, my mom blows her nose hard and wipes away a constant flow of tears. *Sucker*, I think, even though I'd cried when Wilson left for college the day before, ignoring his flaws and sobbing instead over the unfairness of being abandoned in this mess.

I call Laura and beg her to pick me up so we can drive to the beach. I'm outside before she can even honk. Freedom courses through my body as I breathe out the sick, stale air of my house and breathe in the cold shock of winter. I sink into the familiar cushion of her passenger seat and we drive in silence for a while, comforted by the familiar Long Island landmarks of diners, drugstores, and shopping centers that blur by as Laura steers confidently over the drawbridge to Long Beach.

Driving slowly along the beach parking lot—in the winter we rarely exit the car or see the actual beach—Laura hesitantly asks, "Marisa, how's your mom? How are you doing?"

I stiffen. Dodging the question, I gripe about my brother and his kiss-up routine, and relay how sad it was to say goodbye to Wilson. Laura nods sympathetically. I relax. These are the things we know how to talk about: asshole brothers, confusing boyfriends. No one has taught us how to talk about a dying mother. It is a foreign language. Laura's willing to test out the new vocabulary, the words falling clumsily off her tongue, but I know it's only because she's far enough removed. It's not *her* mother. My words are stuck with my emotions in that volcanic space beneath the surface—a zone I can't even access, let alone allow her into. What phrases would even describe how my mom is doing, how I'm doing? And wouldn't words just make this whole thing real, when it can't be, it just can't be. Sentences struggle to emerge, but I won't let them. I swallow and swallow and swallow them back down, a reflex that will soon become second nature.

"Just know I'm here for you, OK?" Laura says. I nod, fighting back tears.

Laura drives me home, and I study my house from her car. It's weird, but ever since the diagnosis, my house just doesn't *look* the same. The brown shingles that once seemed so homey now look faded and worn. The trees that once framed our split-level now seem to shroud us from the public eye. The shades are drawn, no flecks of warm light peeking through. It has transformed into a death house. I wish I didn't have to go in, but I have nowhere else to go; this is my home. I slip in quietly and go straight to my room.

When Monday finally comes, I feel relieved. School lets out at 2:20 p.m. each day, but I find a reason to stay. When the bell rings, I head for the yearbook staff room. Natalie and I sit together, cutting out photos and arranging them in collages. We make sure to include tons of photos of our friends and "misplace" the ones of popular kids. All afternoon I eat snack after snack from the vending machine, stuffing down my feelings with each salty bite. At 6 p.m., I drive Natalie home and open my front door just in time for dinner, never more grateful for *Seinfeld* reruns replacing the need for conversation. The only thing that annoys me is the laugh track. I used to think I'd be the perfect person to record, since I laugh at anything; now I think, who are these idiots who laugh so easily? Obviously they've never had anything *real* happen to them. After scarfing down my food and going back for seconds, I head directly to my room and shut my door. I call Tony and we chat for three hours, fantasizing about our band becoming famous and taking *Seventeen* quizzes. Sometimes Mom calls down or knocks on my door, and in an annoyed voice I huff, "I'm on the phone," and that usually gets her to leave me alone. I don't emerge from my room until the house is asleep, and then I go online to talk to Wilson. He never asks about my mom, and, honestly, I'm half-mad, half-relieved. It's another place in my life where I can make it all disappear. Sometime between midnight and 2 a.m., I shut off my lights and cocoon beneath my covers.

On some level, I know I'm avoiding The Stuff With My Mom, but my body is telling me *go go go*, and the momentum feels wild and addictive, draining only when I pass out each night. Days go by before I realize that I've stopped going upstairs to my parents' room, as if by some magical power I've killed her off already. That should be terrifying, but instead it feels empowering. Maybe because at this point anything seems better than waiting two months for the inevitable.

Marisa / **Sally**

*G*od, *please cure me*, I beg each night. Silent prayers as my husband snores beside me. In the past, his snoring has been one of my biggest pet peeves. "Billy, I'm gonna shove a sock in your mouth!" I'd often hissed when his gutteral growls kept me awake. "Sal, what do you want from me?" he'd mumble groggily, then roll over and fall back to sleep. Now I let it slide. This poor man who might have a dying wife. Who am I to stop his snores?

Everyone seems to have an escape plan. Bill disappears into sleep. Jordan is miles away in college, but calls each day and seems relieved just to hear my voice. Missy holes herself up in her room or downstairs at the computer, or goes out with friends. I waiver between understanding her needs and feeling abandoned. It's a lot for a teenager to process, I remind myself. I try to give her space to come back to me in her own time, when she is ready. But a small voice keeps asking, *what if it's too late*?

Escaping is impossible for me. At night, when I should be sleeping, I'm too busy praying. I pray and pray like I haven't prayed since I was a little girl attending yeshiva in New Haven, Connecticut. Mostly, I pray for my upcoming appointment with Dr. Bruckner. In the days between my diagnosis and my appointment with him, I live on death row. It feels like he's my only source of hope, my final plea bargain to remain on this earth with my family and my friends and my job—my *life*.

The problem is I don't even know when my appointment will be. When I first call Dr. Bruckner, his receptionist fits me in right away. However, she informs me I first need to schedule a biopsy at the hospital. Well, this turns into quite the ordeal. "I can schedule you in three weeks," the receptionist at the hospital says, clearly giving me the cold shoulder. I request that the doctor performing the biopsy call me back. When he calls a few days later, I explain my diagnosis and ask him if the appointment can be moved up. He hesitates. I say, kindly but firmly: "If I were your wife, would you make me wait three weeks?" He says he'll see me this week.

In comparison, the biopsy itself is far less challenging—unpleasant but uneventful. Afterward I pace the house for days, waiting for the phone to ring, until finally Dr. Bruckner's receptionist calls to tell me the biopsy results are in and I can come see Dr. Bruckner tomorrow. In the morning I call in sick to work, an easier excuse than explaining what might actually be wrong. My only guilt is for my students. Learning disabilities plague them, and the school rarely ever hires a special ed sub, which means when I'm absent they miss out on the services they so desperately need.

"Mr. Ciani probably couldn't find anyone willing to teach in the dungeon," Bill jokes on the car ride there. Mr. Ciani is the very-obviously-toupeed principal of my school, and the dungeon is my classroom: a basement room with exposed pipes and barred windows located next to the custodian's quarters. Bill only teases me about it because he knows a part of me has grown to adore the Queens elementary school over the twelve years I've taught there. If I die, who'll teach my kids? Who'll reward their hard work by letting them bring in their favorite music to dance to for the last ten minutes of class every Friday? "You like rap music, Mrs. Bardach?" the kids ask me. "I like all kinds of music," I lie, then press play and watch these amazingly resilient students shake their nonexistent hips to the hip-hop beats. My kids. I can't leave them hanging.

Driving to the hospital takes an hour, but in many ways it feels like a normal workday, since Bill typically drives us to work in Queens, dropping me off at my school and picking me up at the end of the day. We've done this for years. All of our off-hours—before and after school, weekends, vacations, summers—are spent together. We even spent last year together taking a sabbatical to learn about computer software at LaGuardia College. Our class congratulated us on our ability to stay together and live through a sabbatical year. They said their marriages would not have survived that closeness.

With us, it's just the opposite. We enjoy being together, even though at home we spend our time in different rooms doing different things. But we miss each other when we're not together.

Before I know it, Bill and I are in Dr. Bruckner's office. This time I don't wait for nightfall to pray. I talk to God so much I'm surprised he doesn't scold me, "Pipe down, Sally." I guess he knows how much I need him.

Dr. Bruckner looks different than I expect. First of all, he's a religious Jew and wears a *yarmulke* and *tzitzit* (the small head covering and tassels you sometimes see dangling out of a man's overcoat). A long gray beard covers half his face, leaving only his bushy eyebrows and squinty eyes as means by which to gauge his facial expressions. I find his appearance comforting. He could easily be any of the Orthodox men I grew up around, the grandfathers who walked to synagogue on the Sabbath alongside my family.

Bill and I sit nervously as Dr. Bruckner studies my CAT scan and the report about my liver biopsy. Finally, he looks up at us, his gaze settling on me.

"Sally, you have Stage 4 pancreatic cancer," he says gravely.

Hearing it said out loud in such a matter-of-fact way feels so final, so hopeless. Hot tears drip down my cheekbones and, as always, my nose starts running. I blow loudly into a tissue and try to compose myself so I can listen. A friend forewarned that I must become my own best health advocate and suggested I write down everything. "No, really, *everything*," she'd cautioned. Dutifully, I reach into my purse and pull out a navy blue Mead notebook. It's one of Missy's leftover school notebooks from her Health class. I stare at the word "Health" scrawled on the cover in White-Out pen in her girlish handwriting. Sarcastically, I wonder if I should edit her label—shouldn't it read "Unhealthy"? Focusing my attention back on the doctor, I try to write down everything he's saying.

There are four stages of cancer, Dr. Bruckner explains. Stage 1 is the best; Stage 4 is the worst. Mine is at Stage 4 because it has spread to my liver and is now inoperable—but not untreatable. Dr. Zinberg wasn't wrong: because pancreatic cancer is often discovered so late, many patients don't make it past six months. But even though his diagnosis is similar to Dr. Zinberg's, Dr. Bruckner is far more optimistic.

"I've kept patients alive for ten years," Dr. Bruckner says. "You'll be on chemo every two to three weeks for the rest of your life. It won't be easy. But your job is to stick around until we find a cure."

That's when Bill and I discover that maybe I have a chance to beat this horrible disease. Because the cancer has spread, I'm no longer eligible for the Whipple surgery, an extensive operation that seems to link organs and ducts that certainly don't belong together. I'm disappointed by this, as I'd hoped for a "quick fix," but Dr. Bruckner doesn't make me feel hopeless. I can tell he's a nonconformist and an unusual doctor. I immediately like and trust him. He's bright—I could see that when he was viewing my CAT scan pictures, concentrating so intensely on such small images. I know I'm in good hands. He has a gruff, asthmatic voice, much like Marlon Brando as the Godfather, and he makes me an offer I couldn't refuse: I'm going to battle this disease, have a positive outlook. He orders: "Always keep your chin up."

Of course, like most cancer patients, one of my first questions is vain: "Am I going to lose my hair?"

"Unlikely," he says. I know it's the least of my worries, but still, I hope he's right.

Back in the car, heading home from the appointment with Bill, I'm beginning to feel optimistic until the worst part of what he says hits me: I'll have to stop teaching. Chemotherapy will weaken my immune system, the doctor said, and catching colds and bugs from my students will only set back my progress. I have my own children to think about—Jordan and Missy—and I have to put them first. I call Mr. Ciani the next morning. Even though he's so peculiar, always yelling my last name "Bardach!" to signal me to come into his office to chat, he sounds shell-shocked when I tell him my news. I can't even risk returning to say goodbye—what would I say anyway?—and I ask him to please tell my students. Most have had such miserable family lives, and I feel terribly guilty at the thought of being yet another adult who abandons them.

A gruff voice echoes in my head: "Always keep your chin up." Dr. Bruckner's words of wisdom. I don't cry when I call Mr. Ciani, nor when I hang up. Doctor's orders—and I obey.

CHAPTER 3
Treatment

Marisa / Sally

S hit! I curse as the front door of my house creaks open. *I hope she didn't hear me.*

Gently, gently, I close the door behind me and slowly turn the lock. The click seems to echo down the front hallway and up the stairs. *Did she hear me?*

I peer up at the stairs to my bedroom. Six stairs. I can do this. Placing one careful foot at a time, lurking like a burglar, I beg the stairs not to groan under the thick rubber soles of my black Mary Janes. I should've taken them off; socks would be quieter. Must remember that for next time.

Movement upstairs. The bedsprings hiccup. *Did she hear me?*

Hiccup, hiccup go the springs again, squeaking under my mom's shifting weight. Tip-toeing up the stairs, I picture her lounging on her side of the bed, propped up by one fat and one skinny pillow, reading by the dim yellow lamp, legs wrapped in her faded cotton brown blanket.

One more step. Just one more and then I'll be safe. I lift up my left leg.

"Miss?" she calls out from her bedroom.

Busted.

Sneaking around has become my afternoon routine. When both my parents worked, I had the house to myself for at least an hour after school. Usually I'd watch MTV, eat Wheat Thins smothered in Skippy Reduced Fat Super Chunk Peanut Butter, and put off starting my homework. But being sick forced Mom to retire, so now she stays home alone every day and seems to pounce on me as soon as I walk in the door: "How was your day? Did you get a lot of homework? You know you have to finish it before you watch *Dawson's Creek*. Are you hungry? Do you want me to fix you a snack?" She's so annoying!

So I try to slip into the house without her noticing—which is nearly impossible, since she's so eager to spend time together and chitchat about life or try to get me to open up about her being sick. I used to love our talks, but not anymore. What were once intimate talks about life are now intimate talks about death, and I can't handle the switch. Every nerve in my body starts to rattle, screaming at me to run away from her. Now, far, fast, go, go, GO!

Realizing I haven't responded to her, I call in an irritated voice, "Hi Mom," and then close my bedroom door loudly enough for her to get the memo that I don't want to be disturbed.

I could have—should have—walked upstairs to her room, said hi, and hugged her. Asked, "How was your day, Mom?" like we're the Brady Bunch family. I know that's what Mom and Dad want me to do. It all feels so fake, though. Why bother when she'll be dead in two months? *Fuck*, it's already February—could she really only have *one month* left? One month is nothing. One month is like she's already gone.

No, I decide. I'm definitely not telling any of my friends the news about my mom except for Laura. Let them find out after the fact. It's better than having the whole school gossip about me until then, circling like vultures.

I take off my messenger bag and haul it onto the bed. It's a shiny black nylon bag with silver clasps, like a fancy adult's briefcase. "Mom, look, isn't it nice?" I said at the Gap last fall. "And it's on sale," I continued, knowing that would sell her. Not only did she buy one for me, but she bought the same one for herself. It became her work bag, though now it just sits slumped in her closet alongside a rainbow of unworn work clothes.

Checking out my own outfit in the full-length mirror, I worry all those after-school snack binges are going straight to my butt. Oh well. I sigh as I slide off my Mary Janes, kicking them toward the corner of the room, next to my extra-long twin sheets for college. I'd ordered the shoes and sheets from the Delia's catalog—something my mom rarely allows. My room is a mess, but the sheets are still perfectly pressed in the unopened clear package. Royal blue flannel with red and yellow stars, as if the right sheets will broadcast my cool status. *Look at me! I'm the drummer chick you're dying to be friends with!* Now it seems so shallow. What if I can't even go away to college? I wonder if Delia's accepts returns if your mom dies.

School was so stupid today, with everyone blabbering on and on about Valentine's Day coming up. "Do you think it's cheesy to wear red?" Hailee asked me in band, eyes wide as if it were a life-or-death question. I shrugged, smiled. *I might wear black every day of my life*, I felt like shouting. I just wanted to get through the day so I could go home. But I forgot what home meant: *she* was there.

I still can't believe she retired. The risk of catching colds from the kids is too great, she claims, but I think it's the fear of facing everyone and admitting she's sick. Having to look them in the eye every day. Better to have them remember her as she was: healthy, happy, normal. Sometimes I envy her coworkers and students; they don't have to witness what happens between now and then. I try to picture my mom switching from vibrant and healthy to some movie-like scene of her slipping from consciousness in a hospital bed. But all I can see is Susan Sarandon in *Stepmom* and Sally Field in *Forrest*

Gump, actresses with too much pancake makeup dying a Hollywood death—not my mom dying in the real world. A sick feeling comes over me, and I shake the thought away.

Homework, I tell myself, *I should do homework.* I grab a greedy handful of Sour Patch Kids from my bag and turn on my TV, quickly lowering the volume to eleven. Normal volume is about thirty, but eleven is loud enough for me to hear and low enough for my parents *not* to hear. Mom likes me to finish my homework before watching TV, but I've secretly watched *Saved by the Bell* every day at 5 p.m. for the past few years. I rarely get caught.

Yes! My favorite episode: Zach and Kelly's Prom! Kelly's dad loses his job, so she can't afford to buy a dress, but Zach plans a private prom in her backyard with a big banner that says "Zach & Kelly's Prom." And then they slow dance and Kelly looks so pretty with her wispy brown hair and cutoff sweatshirt that falls off one shoulder. I wonder what kind of dress I'll get for prom. It's hard to believe it's already February, and that prom is only four months away. But then I remember Mom will be dead. Will I even go to prom? Or will I just boycott it all—prom, graduation, college, life? It's hard to imagine everyday life even existing without her. My brain feels like a CD that keeps skipping every time it gets to the best part of the song, but I can't bring myself to just skip to the next track. I'm stuck. And all I want is to go back to the beginning, before all this happened.

I take out my math notebook and open my textbook. Calculus, ugh. Get ready to suck. I flip through my planner to find the assignment: *p134, #2-24, evens.* Great. I write out the problems, then do the first step or two of each one. *This is impossible.* I could call Laura for help. She's so much better at Calc than I am. But then she'll ask a million questions about my mom.

Lately, when Laura calls the house and my mom picks up the phone, they talk for, like, an *hour.* I hear my mom's cheerful phone voice say, "Hi Laura!" And from my mom's hushed tone after that, I know they're talking about me, and that my mom's asking Laura a million questions about how I'm dealing with her being sick. An hour later my mom yells, "Missy! Laura's on the phone!" and I pick up and say, "How long have you guys been talking for?!" in a jokingly accusatory tone, as if I was totally unaware of their conversation. I'm pretty good at playing dumb.

The truth is, I don't really mind that Laura and my mom talk about me. Secretly, I'm kind of glad they're worried about me. I'm worried about me, too. And them talking to each other is easier than me having to talk. Plus, they adore each other. Somehow, even when Laura comes over on a Friday night, my mom winds up sitting on my bed chatting with us.

"I'm coming back in my next life with your hourglass figure," my mom always says as Laura frowns at her reflection in my full-length mirror.

"Sally, stop. You're a toothpick. I'd kill for your body," Laura always responds.

I used to like just sitting on my bed and listening to their funny banter, but it's not like that anymore. Laura hasn't even been to our house since Mom was diagnosed, since all I ever want to do is leave.

I decide I won't call Laura for Calc. Mr. MacMullen knows I suck anyway. I just pray he won't ask us to hand in our homework tomorrow. Every time he does that, I cringe. He better not fail me. Maybe I should drop the class.

A toilet flush upstairs startles me. Then, soft padded footsteps on the stairs. *Fuck.*

I reach over and press the power button on the TV. Zach and Kelly vanish. I pretend to look absorbed in my Calc homework as she knocks on my door.

"Come in," I say in a flat voice.

She opens the door tentatively and stands in the doorway. I don't look up.

"Hi, Miss," she says.

"Hi." I punch meaningless numbers into my calculator, hoping she'll get the hint.

"What're you working on?" she asks, peering over at my books.

"Calc." 2+2, I tap into my TI-83 graphing calculator.

"I'm going to make spaghetti and meatballs for dinner," she says, knowing it's my favorite. "Does that sound good?"

"Yeah, fine, Mom. I need to finish this."

"Oh, all right. I'll let you be. Dinner should be ready around seven."

"Can you shut my door?"

Click. Safe. I put down my pencil and stare at my calculator. I know Mom and Dad are sick of my "avoidance routine," as I overheard them call it the other day. "She'll come around in her own time," Mom reassured Dad. *Don't hold your breath*, I felt like telling them. Her new doctor says he's kept patients alive for ten years. I haven't met him, but I don't believe him. I've heard that doctors do anything to try to boost their patients' spirits. That thinking positively can help keep them alive. Yeah right. If they want to have faith in him, fine, but I'm not going to get sucked into his lies. The two-month prognosis is still burned into my brain, and diminishing by the day. I try to figure out more math problems, but the numbers seem to taunt me: two, one, zero. I slide the lid back on the calculator. I have my answer.

The phone rings and jolts me from my thoughts. I bet it's Laura.

"Missyyyy!" My mom yells. "Phooooone!"

I pick up. "Hey."

"Hey, Marisa? It's Tony."

"Oh, hi!" I say. He calls almost every night, but I'm always surprised to hear his voice. We still laugh about the first time he called me, because I thought for sure he was kicking me out of the band. After all, I'd never been in a real band before, with weekly rehearsals and shows at venues throughout Long Island. What if I wasn't as good as their last drummer? But he was only calling to ask me out to lunch with the guys. That was a few months ago, but now it feels like

I've known them forever. I love how they accept me into their group, and never treat me different just because I'm the only girl or the newcomer. But Tony is still the only one who ever calls me, and I wonder if the other guys know. Something about our conversations feels secretive from them, from Wilson, from the whole world. It's like entering a private universe.

"What's up?" he says now.

"Nothing really. I can't do Calc for the life of me."

"Man, high school sucks."

"You're lucky you're done with it," I say wistfully, wishing I had graduated with him two years earlier. I try to picture us walking down the high school halls, hand in hand, that cute couple who formed a band together and fell in love. I'm not sure if I even see him that way, or if I just like the story.

"So, you down for practice tomorrow?"

"Yeah! Definitely."

"You're doing a good job…getting the hang of it," he says.

"Oh, thanks. I hope so. I still feel like the new kid."

"Marisa, are you crazy? You're-a-crazy!" he says, imitating a thick Italian accent. He doesn't have to try very hard; he *is* Italian. At first I thought his accent was weird, but when we spoke for an hour a few nights ago, I started thinking it was cute.

"Seriously, *sweethawt*," he continues, now imitating the music store owner who insisted on calling me that when I bought drumsticks with Tony last week.

"That guy was so gross!" I giggle, remembering the hairy store owner.

"*Sweethawt, you really play the drums? Like a full set?*" Tony mimicks.

"Ewwww!" I squeal. "What did he think I played? The flute?"

"I can't picture you ever playing the flute," Tony says.

"My mom wanted me to," I say.

"Seriously?"

"Yeah. In fourth grade they make you choose what instrument you want to play. My mom was like, 'How about the flute or the clarinet, Missy?' I said, 'How am I gonna take my anger out on a flute, Mom? I want to play the drums—like Jordan.' I always wanted to do everything my brother did."

"What were you so angry about? You were in fourth grade!"

"Actually...I have no idea!" I laugh, because it's too soon to be serious with him. But inside I know I *was* angry, even then, at age nine. I wonder if it's because my emotions have always been bubbling under the surface, and drums were a way for them to get out. They still are.

"Well, it's a good thing you chose drums."

"Yeah."

"Otherwise we never woulda met."

"Aw, Tony! I...I know!" I stammer and feel myself blush.

My mom calls from the kitchen. "Missyyyy! Can you come set the table?"

"Just a sec," I yell.

"Do you have to go?" Tony asks.

"No, no, it's fine."

"You sure?"

"Yeah. Where were we?"

"I don't remember."

"Oh." I say, disappointed. I want to go back to that moment with him, but it's gone.

"So I'll see you tomorrow, *sweethawt*?" he says.

"Definitely. Are you gonna come out for lunch?"

Lately, the only fun part of school was when Tony came out to lunch. The four of us from the band and whoever else was around piled into two cars and drove to Wendy's or Burger King to consume way too many fries and debate the merits of dunking them in ketchup versus barbecue sauce (I defend the latter). Last time, Tony grabbed a spare napkin and drew a caricature of me in a bikini popping out of a birthday cake. He's in college for animation, so of course he's really good at drawing, but I was surprised that he made me look hot! I'd laughed so they wouldn't notice I was blushing, but his picture made me wonder if he sees me the way I've always wanted to be seen.

"I think so," he says. "Are you coming out?"

"Yeah, I think so."

"Well then, I'll see you then."

Another call from downstairs, this time my dad: "Missy! Come help your mother."

"Five minutes," I call back.

"Not in five minutes...NOW!!!"

I cringe and cover the mouthpiece with my hand, hoping Tony didn't hear my dad's roar.

"Do you have to go?" Tony asks.

"No, it's fine. Well, yeah, I guess. I have to set the table. But I can wait..."

"Go ahead. You want me to call you later? Will you be around?"

"Yeah, I'll be—" Beep. Call waiting. I better take it in case it's a doctor for Mom. "Tony, can you hang on a second?"

"Yeah, sure, no problem."

I click the receiver. "Hello?"

"How's your mom?" Laura asks.

"Oh, hi. Um, she's fine. She's making dinner."

"When does she start chemo?"

"I, um, actually have to go set the table. And Tony's on the other line. Can I call you after?"

"Yeah. Call me back, though."

"I will."

"Promise?"

"Yes! Geez!"

I hang up, already scheming how to avoid the Mom topic with Laura when I call her later. I click back, relieved to return to a conversation that's ridiculous and fun. A place I can hide. "Tony?"

"*Sweethawt*, yup, I'm here."

"I should really go. My parents are going to kill me. Do you mind?"

"Ma-ris-a," he says, faking a serious tone. "That's it. You're outta the band."

"Tony!" I giggle.

"Talk to you later, *sweethawt*."

"Bye!"

I'm still giggling when I hang up. Oh, Tony. He's so funny.

I close my Calc textbook and put my notebook back in my bag. When I go to the bathroom to wash my hands, my face in the mirror is flushed and still smiling. I think about lunch tomorrow and smile again. *Marisa, you have a boyfriend*, I scold myself. *Remember? Wilson? Tall Asian guy?* But right now he seems far away, geographically and otherwise.

I head downstairs. Marinara sauce perfumes the kitchen. As I fumble in the drawer for forks, spoons, and knives, avoiding eye contact with still-kinda-pissed-off Dad, I peek over at Mom stirring sauce on the stove.

Gray capri sweats and an oversize Susan B. Anthony T-shirt hang on her 104-pound, five-foot-one body. My dad always brings her leftover shirts that read Susan B. Anthony, the name of the junior high school where he's a guidance counselor. Once, a few years ago, I'd sat on my mom's bed, chatting with her as she settled down after work. The first thing she did was take off her blouse and bra and put on one of those T-shirts.

"Ahh!" she'd sighed dreamily. "This is my favorite part of the day—taking off my bra!"

Having a mere A cup, I don't fully understand, but I hope one day I'll develop a C cup like her, and feel that same sense of relief and contentment when removing my bra. She says her boobs got bigger after she had kids, so I'm pretty sure mine will, too. They'd better.

Now that she stays in her pajamas all day, she never wears a bra. But as I look over at her, stirring the sauce and maybe wondering if this is the last time she'll ever make meatballs for her family, her breasts seem to sag under her T-shirt, as if to say, "Who would've thought we'd miss wearing a bra?"

Marisa / **Sally**

Breast cancer runs in my family. It was February 22, 1957—my fourteenth birthday—when my mother discovered a lump under her arm while hanging laundry on the outside clothesline. She came in, sat down on a kitchen chair, and cried, "I have cancer."

My older brother Stuart, who was seventeen, passed out. My younger brother Howie, only twelve, stood in the background. We revived Stu and my mother composed herself, calling the doctor and making an appointment.

The doctor told her it was breast cancer and she would need surgery. "If you were a man, I'd tell you to go home and get your affairs in order," he told her, because back then men handled all the financial paperwork and money.

Surgery was scheduled for three weeks from that day because that's when they could get a hospital bed. A few days later my family was in the car on a Sunday and my mom was so nervous, she was crying. "I can't wait three weeks," she kept saying.

My maternal grandmother had died of cancer when my mom was ten years old. I was named after her. My mom always talked about her and every year cried at her gravesite. Maybe that's what gave my mom the courage to call the doctor and assert herself: "I cannot and will not wait three weeks. Get me into the hospital now." She went almost immediately. My father called the doctor the night before the surgery, and he told my dad it was very serious. My dad looked like he might faint. I suddenly realized it was my mom who was emotionally strong—the glue that held our family together.

My mom survived the surgery, though she lost a breast. I felt like my own breast had been cut off. I was just turning into a young woman myself, and it hit me very hard. I didn't see her the night of the surgery. Her relatives went, but somehow I didn't go, like they were sparing me. But they weren't. My Aunt Lil, my mother's sister, went to visit her and came back to my house crying and telling me everything would be all right. If that was so, then why was she crying?

The next day I definitely was going to see her. Meanwhile, I was going to school—ninth grade—working hard, cooking for my family (something I really didn't know how to do), cleaning the house (also something I never did), going to dancing school and Hebrew school, and praying all the time. Finally I went to see my mom. "Doll!" she exclaimed, her special name for me, which I now call Missy. Her chest was wrapped in bandages, but she was sitting up in bed, talking and smiling. She had a smile that could light up a room. That day it lit up my heart.

Finally she came home. Meanwhile I had developed a nervous cough—I would never stop coughing, even into my adult life. Some of my relatives were over the day she came home, and they took over the cooking. I ran outside to play baseball with my brothers. I felt my freedom come back. My mom was honest with me. They removed her breast and some lymph nodes from under her arm. If she could remain cancer-free for five years, she would be OK. She stayed in bed for one day. Then she was up and around like nothing had ever happened. And she was cheerful and full of hope and love. She was as loving to me as she always had been. I never stopped praying for her. And I knew exactly when the five years was up. I kept track. I would say to myself, "When would I be old enough to take care of myself? If she lived until I was eighteen, would I be strong enough then?" I continually questioned myself—usually at night. She was my strength, my hope, my love, my life, my childhood, my innocence.

I was her support group. No chemo then, no radiation, just a radical mastectomy, prayer, and hope. I went with her for prosthetic fittings. People knew about her. It was New Haven, Connecticut, and she belonged to Young Israel, an Orthodox community, although we lived in a mixed neighborhood of mostly Jews and Catholics. When we were downtown, she'd run into someone and they'd have a conversation, and then when the person walked away, she'd say to me, "She was staring at me." She wasn't a paranoid person. She was correct. It was before breast cancer was publicized and we didn't hear of women having mastectomies. So my mother had become an oddity to a few ignorant people. I would say to her, "Ma—they're stupid. Just ignore them!"

This four-foot-eleven-inch, hundred-pound, beautiful woman would become my hero. She was my best friend and would remain so for the rest of her life, living well into her seventies, sadly passing away just after Missy was born.

I don't know how my mom kept it together. Agitated the night before my first chemo session, I try everything to fall asleep. I watch reruns of *Seinfeld* and *Everybody Loves Raymond*. I read the latest Danielle Steel novel I took out from the library. I relax every part of my body and take deep breaths—a trick my old therapist taught me in my twenties, and one I often used with Missy when she was little and couldn't sleep. "Relax your toes, relax your toes. Relax your ankles, relax your ankles," I'd repeat in a meditative voice, calming all her tiny body parts until, at last, she'd fall asleep.

Missy. My little night owl. Maybe she's still up. Bill's snoring stops as I inch off the bed. I eye him, half-hoping I woke him up. A few pats on the head might be all I need to fall into a peaceful slumber. A second later, the blustering snores I've slept next to for the past twenty-two years resume. I open the bedroom door and peek from the landing downstairs to Missy's room. Dim light shines out from under her door. *Yes, she's up!*

As I pad down the stairs, her room goes dark. I knock softly. "Miss?" I whisper. "Missy?" Nothing.

I walk downstairs to the kitchen and heat a mug of water in the microwave. Lipton Lemon Soother is my favorite, and tea seems like it could cure insomnia (decaf, of course). As the microwave hums, I study the kitchen. Bill and I remodeled it a few years earlier. We hired workers to strip the '70s wallpaper and replace the dark wood cabinets. Weekends became scavenger hunts for tile, paint, Formica counters, a new fridge, stove, and sink. We were a dynamic design duo: I researched the stores; Bill drove and navigated. We studied tones of "almond" and "beige" until our eyes blurred. Then we brought home samples to hold up and ask Missy and Jordan what they thought. Jordan didn't care unless he thought something was "disgusting" or "ugly." Missy shrugfully chose her favorites, but mostly for the potential fame of selecting the winner. I look around, pleased. We built a beautiful kitchen.

Beep, beep, beep, the microwave sounds. My tea is ready. I slide on my socks around the kitchen, pretending to be Oksana Baiul. Missy and I loved watching her figure skate in the Olympics. She was our favorite, with her Ukrainian accent and cute blond ponytail, practically tap dancing on the ice.

I dunk my tea bag, add honey, and walk into the den. I sit in my chair at the dining room table. It's funny how family furniture gets assigned seating. Even though Bill is such a family man, my seat is at the head of the table. *Empty chairs at empty tables*—the lyrics from *Les Miserables* haunt me. In two months, will my kids have an empty chair at their table? I put down my mug, touch my hand to my forehead, and sob to my sleeping family, repeating in my head: *I'm sorry, I'm sorry, I'm so so sorry.*

In the car on the way to the hospital the next day, Bill places a hand on top of my head and pets my hair, like he does sometimes when he senses I'm anxious. I smile weakly at him, then turn my eyes back to the window. *He's driving me to my first chemotherapy treatment*, I remind myself, trying to believe it. Maybe this is all just a nightmare, and when I wake up…

"You OK, Sal?" Bill asks.

"Just tired," I say quickly. I'm afraid if I mention chemo or cancer, he might start sobbing and have to pull over, like he did the night I was diagnosed. I'll do anything to keep him from feeling that pain again. "I couldn't sleep last night."

"I thought you left the room," Bill says, switching lanes. "You could've woken me up."

"No, you have such a long day today. Driving me to the hospital, and then going to work. I couldn't do that to you."

"Did you go down to Missy?"

"I tried to, but she was asleep, or maybe just pretending to be. I think she's still in shock from all this…"

"She's not being there for you, Sal," Bill counters. "She's being selfish. And I don't like it."

"She's just adjusting," I say, defending little Missy, even though I know he's speaking the truth. I'm surprised and hurt by her reaction, too, but mostly just lonesome for the friendship we once had. I know Bill's anger is just because he misses her, too.

Poor Bill. He's taken the diagnosis so hard. I retired immediately, but Bill, only fifty-four, wants to continue working. I think it's good for him—he'll have a distraction from my illness—but today, for a brief, selfish minute, I wish he had the day off so he could spend it with me.

I hate hospitals. But Dr. Bruckner told me I'll have to go to the hospital for chemo every three weeks for the rest of my life, or until they find a cure for pancreatic cancer. I'm glad it's not hopeless, believe me, but for me, hospital visits are the worst punishment they could choose. *One day at a time, Sal*, I comfort myself, but I can't relax.

Bill turns off the traffic news and switches to a rock station. I continue looking out the window. Trees border the highway, and I think of Connecticut. I wish my parents were still alive. Being sick always makes me feel like a little kid, even as an adult, even with kids of my own. Something instinctual within me craves my mom's kind eyes and soothing touch. Without parents, there's no one to calm my worries. Who can I confide in about this cancer? Whenever I call my relatives and friends, I always wind up comforting *them*. I need someone to comfort *me*.

We pull into the parking lot of St. Luke's-Roosevelt hospital on the Upper West Side of Manhattan, and my heart beats faster and faster. It only gets worse as Bill and I fill out miles of paperwork. When I finally get assigned to a room, the doctors have to give me Ativan to calm me down. Then they hook me up to a machine that administers various chemo drugs over a twenty-four-hour period.

The first day, I'm so scared that Bill stays with me and doesn't go to work. I feel bad, but I'm secretly relieved. But quickly I realize that crying or being scared won't help me. Dr. Bruckner tells me chemo will become my friend. It will keep me alive. I have to embrace what was always so scary for me: hospitals, doctors, nurses, aides, etc. Nurses become my best friends as they are my caretakers day and night.

Soon I become used to the hospital life routine: eating breakfast at 7:40 a.m., going to the bathroom with my "dancing partner" (IV stand), being woken up all night to take my temperature. I'm no longer scared, and chemo isn't as bad as I expected. The next time, I'll send Bill to work and know that I'll be all right.

When I leave the next day, I realize I've become part of the circle of cancer fighters—the patients who live on chemo and radiation. I make up my mind rather quickly. I will survive.

CHAPTER 4

The Dress

Marisa / Sally

It will be maroon. My favorite color. Maroon with spaghetti straps and a cowl neckline that makes it look like you have cleavage, even when you don't. Maybe a bow. No, not a bow. A ruffle. Crap, I messed up. I scribble over my drawing with blue pen and sketch a new one. This one has a ruffle.

"Your paper on *The Awakening* is due on Friday," Mr. Minor announces. Everyone begins to put their books in their bags. "Hey! The bell hasn't rung yet. You still have five full minutes. *Don't* pack up."

I add strappy platform sandals and a necklace to go with my dress. Writing that paper is going to suck. I've only read half the book, even though AP English is my favorite subject. I love Mr. Minor, too, with his flamboyant antics, sophisticated style and culture, and brilliant mind. He went to Columbia University and now lives in Manhattan, commuting each day to our high school in Long Island. I liked to picture his fancy evenings: popping into a jazz club, having intellectual debates with friends, or writing the next great American novel. I wonder if I'll have such a glamorous life one day.

Until then, I'll have to speed-read the book and somehow write that paper. Lately, with The Stuff With My Mom, it's been hard to concentrate on any of my school work, let alone some feminist novel from a million years ago.

And today it's especially hard to focus: I'm going prom dress shopping after school.

Mom suggested it over the weekend. I was running out the door to go to Laura's when she called to me, "Miss?" I opened the front door. Maybe I could pretend I didn't hear her and make a run for it. The door creaked. "Miss!" she snapped.

"What?!" I demanded.

"Do you have anything on Monday after school?" she asked.

Tuesday was Yearbook. Wednesday was Model Congress. Thursday was band practice. I didn't have anything on Mondays. And she *knew* it.

"No..." I dawdled.

"Daddy and I want to take you prom dress shopping."

I looked down at my car keys, swinging from their red lanyard. I knew why she was doing this. It was February. *No one* goes prom dress shopping in February. But when everyone went in March and April, she'd be dead.

I tried to think of an excuse. *Laura and I have to study for Calc together. I have to write my English paper. Prom's been canceled.*

"Sounds good," I said, for her sake.

"Oh good!" she chirped. "I'm so excited. I think we should try Ask Alice first, since that's where we found such pretty dresses last year for Wilson's prom. I'm not even sure you'll find a dress as pretty as that one, with the print and the see-through back..."

"Fine, whatever," I cut her off, annoyed. She was being too perky, acting like everything was normal when obviously it wasn't. She was trying too hard. It was as if she thought that if she were cheerful enough, fun enough, she could pull me back beside her and we'd race off together away from this. Didn't she realize I wasn't a little kid anymore, someone who could be easily cheered up with a Band-Aid and a lollipop and a promise that everything would be OK? For me, it was all passing by in a blur: the too early, prom dress shopping date; the normal prom dress shopping months, when all the moms and daughters would be at the mall together—except us; the actual prom where I'd be clutching my corsage with no mom in sight. I knew for Mom the dress was one bright spot between now and the end. But some of us were going to have to live in the world beyond that, and the early shopping trip was just a lousy reminder. The nerves rattled again, a quiver of rage rising up throughout my body, screaming at me to run. "I gotta go. I'm late."

"Oh, all right, doll," she said, a bit bewildered, as I slammed the door behind me and drove off.

The bell rings. Everyone grabs their bags and rushes out of the classroom. I pack up slowly. *My mom has cancer.* Could I just say that to Mr. Minor? None of my teachers know. And part of me is longing for someone to know, and not just someone but an adult, maybe one who's dealt with this personally and can tell me how to get through it, how it all pans out in the end. The other part of me dreads the daily sympathetic glances, the constant reminders of the reality I don't want to face. School has become my only safe space to be free from it all. The thought of giving up my sacred hiding spot feels like walking through the halls naked. Mr. Minor looks at me.

"Have you heard from any schools yet?" he asks.

"Just Binghamton and Penn State. I'm waiting on the rest."

"You won't have any problem," he reassures me, so proud that I want to study writing. "Keep me updated."

"I will," I promise, smiling and swinging my bag over my shoulder. "Bye, Mr. Minor."

The rest of the day passes slowly, with more classes and prom dress drawings. On the drive home I blast my new favorite band, At the Drive-In, and sing at the top of my lungs. The intense music transports me far from the countless SUVs and traffic lights until I get to the song "Napoleon Solo," about the band's friends who died in a tragic car crash. The lyrics echo my grief. I'm trying so hard to avoid my mom that I've barely even asked about her first chemo treatment. But denial can only distract you to a certain degree. Underneath it all, you know exactly what's going on, and that it's not going away.

When I'm a block away from my house I lower the music. It somehow seems disrespectful to my mom, who's been home all day instead of teaching. Guilt twists my guts, that I've been able to escape to school while she's been forced to retire from hers. I picture her depressed and alone, with too much time on her hands to think about her illness. Dad keeps saying I need to be there for her—whatever that means. But I sit in the car until the song ends and try to ready myself to do that.

When I walk in, some sappy show is on TV and the kitchen smells like toast and jelly. Instead of her usual pajamas, Mom's dressed in Gap overalls and a striped thermal shirt. Lilac eye shadow makes her green eyes dance. She looks pretty. When she comes over for a hug, I don't flinch, like I've been doing lately. Still wearing my coat and my messenger bag, I just hug her and let my eyes well up with tears. I blink quickly before she notices.

"My coat's still on…" I mumble, lifting my puffy arms awkwardly, making her laugh. A diversion, an excuse to pull away. Blinking back tears, I turn to dump my coat by the foot of the stairs, rummaging in my bag for nothing.

"How was your day, doll?" Mom asks brightly, clearly trying to lift the mood. She sits at the kitchen table by the TV, waiting for me to join her. I can tell she hopes we'll chitchat until Dad gets home and we leave to go dress shopping. What we would have done before all this.

"Good," I say, hanging back near the fridge. I'm suddenly starving. But the crackers are on the table—near *her*. I cave. Reaching for a handful of my mom's Saltines (nausea's home remedy) and the jar of peanut butter, I sink into the chair beside her. I pray she'll just keep talking about normal stuff and not about being sick.

"So!" Mom says, swiveling her chair toward me with a warm smile. I can tell she's excited to have her companion back.

"When's Dad coming home?" I ask anxiously, at a loss for other topics. It's a dumb question; he comes home from work at 3:45 p.m. every day.

"Soon," she says, glossing over my fake question. "And then we can leave for the store. Prom dress shopping, here we come!" Using her feet as a spring, Mom rocks back and forth a little in her chair. "Are you excited?"

"Oh, uh, yeah!" I say. In spite of everything, I am. But as soon as I say it, the excitement is replaced by dread. I try to temper my enthusiasm, but it comes out stiff. "I'm curious to see what they have."

Eager to talk, she prattles on about who called her today, especially enthusistic about a woman from her sabbatical. "Everyone's being so nice," she gushes.

"That's nice," I say distractedly. Does she mean that everyone's being so nice *except me*?

I make myself a cracker, thankful for the way the peanut butter sticks to the roof of my mouth, already planning to use that as an excuse to stay mute if Mom asks anything I don't want to answer— like how I'm dealing with everything. Before she even has the chance, I push back my chair and pop up.

"I'm gonna do some homework until we go," I announce, averting my eyes from her hurt expression.

Once upstairs, I blast The Get Up Kids "Holiday" and lay down on my floor. Wilson gave me the CD before he left for the semester, and the songs feel autobiographical, with lyrics about relationships changing when all you want is for them to stay the same. Everyone in my life seems different these days. My mom, once my closest person, who I haven't had a real conversation with in weeks. My dad, who always adored me, now eternally disappointed in me. Laura, my best friend, who I used to laugh with, now always serious, wanting to talk about my mom. Wilson, my first real boyfriend who I liked because he was quiet and weird and different, now lacking because I need him to be so much more. Sometimes I wish everyone would go back to normal. Including me.

I could call Wilson. I could confide in Laura. I could simply walk back downstairs to the kitchen table and say, "Mom, this sucks." Instead I just turn the music louder. It is loneliness of my own doing, but if I undo it, then what? I'm afraid The Stuff With My Mom invades everything. My home life. My school life. My friends. My future. Right now I'm in control. I have safe spaces where it doesn't exist. I can stop it from spreading. But only on the outside. On the inside, the sadness has already traveled throughout my body as fast as my mom's cancer. It takes over more happy cells each day. It bubbles beneath the surface, leaving me constantly on the verge of tears. They leak out now as I close my eyes.

Twenty minutes later, I hear my dad shut the front door and realize I fell asleep. I quickly pat my oily skin with Bonne Bell powder and paint berry gloss on my lips, worried that if I'm late it'll give Dad yet another reason to be mad at me. It's written all over his face. Raised eyebrows when I walk in the door after being at Yearbook all afternoon instead of with Mom. Exasperated sighs when I'm silent during dinner instead of asking Mom how she feels. He wants me to be there for her, and I just…can't. But when I rush downstairs, he greets me playfully: "Monkey!" I'm relieved. Especially on prom dress shopping day, I just want the three of us to get along, like old times. Even if we're pretending.

In the car, Mom complains that the seat hurts her back while Dad tries to steer with one hand and massage her neck with the other. I'm annoyed that even on our prom dress shopping trip, the symptoms of her disease have come to haunt us. Sometimes I wish I were like Wilson's friend Christine, who will probably go to a thrift store alone and casually find some vintage slip dress or an '80s gown with ironic ruffles. No big deal. But my parents raised me to see every little moment as a big deal. Whether we were picking up pizza for dinner (the good kind with the sesame seed crust) or sneaking into a double feature at a movie theater (the good kind with the stadium seating), Mom and Dad made mini moments feel like they mattered. It was my parents' way of showing that we mattered, too.

When Mom dies, who will make me feel like I matter?

I try to picture what it will be like after, just the three of us. I imagine my dad and my brother and me each spinning in a private tornado of grief, without even a way to reach out and see how the other person's doing. Let alone remind each other that we matter.

I gaze out the window at the dirty snow melting in the gutters. *It's not February. It's not February. You're just going prom dress shopping. It doesn't mean anything.*

We park near the store and go inside. It looks different than I remember. When we shopped here last year for a dress for Wilson's prom, the little boutique seemed enchanting. Each dress a possibility, a chance to transform into someone else. Today it just looks like a store, dirty and in disarray, so narrow you can hardly navigate around the circular racks of dresses.

Mom doesn't seem to notice. Smiling broadly, she strides toward the first dress hanging against the wall. "Ooh, Missy! Look at this one." I study the steel gray gown with iridescent sequins and scrunch my nose. It isn't maroon.

She shoves the dress into my arms before I can protest, then scopes out the sales rack while I browse by myself. I choose a Betsy Johnson ruffled party dress, a glamorous red satin sheath, and a maroon-and-black lace gown. The hangers begin to bruise my knuckles.

"I'm gonna go try on," I call out. Dad nods and heads over casually. Mom pushes past the dresses and scurries toward the fitting rooms, not wanting to miss a second.

Before I even try anything on, I study my reflection in the full-length mirror. My face is puffy from overeating and my eyes have that sorrowful stare they've had ever since Mom told us of her diagnosis. But today they have a slight sparkle, too, and I know the old me is excited about dress shopping despite it all. I try to let myself forget and just enjoy the moment.

Taking a breath, I try on the gray dress first. She'll be hurt if I don't. And it's not really my style, so I kind of want to get it out of the way so I can try on the others. But when I step into it, the bottom swirls out like a Cinderella gown and the bodice fits perfectly, even masking the curvier hips and butt that I'm still not used to. I'm almost disappointed, since if it didn't fit, I could reject it without rejecting her.

When I push open the dressing room curtain, Mom and Dad's faces light up. "Oh, Missy, you look beautiful," Mom gushes. "Very pretty," Dad agrees. I step onto the carpeted platform and examine the dress in the fancy three-way mirror. Fluorescent light bounces off the sequins, making the dress sparkle as I turn. It's pretty, in a fairy-tale kind of way, and I like it more than I want to. In the mirror, I see Mom squeeze Dad's hand, and I bask in the feeling of being The Beautiful Daughter Whose Parents Love Her. It's who I've always been, up until now.

I slip on the other dresses, but even the maroon-and-black lace dress doesn't quite match the dress I'd drawn in my notebook. I see a split screen in my head of the fantasy dress and the reality dress. How do I adjust to my new reality? Not just the dress, but everything.

"So…?" Mom asks, bright-eyed. "What do you think?"

She looks so happy, so hopeful. A shiny look I haven't seen in a long time. A hot feeling creeps over me like a fever, and I understand what I have to do. It's the same feeling I used to get on our trips to Florida to see Grandma and Grandpa, when I'd sit between them in the backseat of the car. My soft-spoken, gentle grandfather would put his arm around me, the pointy bones of his wrist digging into my clavicle, his wrinkled hand hanging heavy beside me. *No matter how much it hurts, I won't move*, I'd swear to myself. I knew even a tiny shift would signal my discomfort and cause him to move. And I wanted the reassurance that when he died, I'd know I did the right thing.

I try on the gray gown again. Spotting a potential sale, a pushy saleswoman brings over matching earrings and necklaces. She's annoying, but even I have to admit that the small sparkly beads are a perfect match and make the dress look even prettier. I pile my long curls on top of my head, princess-style. I picture myself stepping out of the limo, reaching for Wilson's hand. Mom isn't there, but I'm wearing the dress she picked out, and that matters.

"OK," I say, taking a deep breath, smiling in a way that looks happy but feels both happy and sad. I know it's a moment we'll all remember, and suddenly I want to get swept up in it. "I'm gonna get it!"

"Ahh, Missy!" Mom screams, clasping her hands together and beaming.

"Mo-om!" I hush her, embarrassed, looking around as if to explain that there are other people in the store, hello?

"What?" She feigns innocence, teasing me. Sometimes I wish I could be as out there as her, so comfortable with expressing whatever I'm feeling right out in the open for everyone to see. "My daughter got a prom dress. It's a big deal!"

I giggle and roll my eyes, teasing her back. She scurries over and embraces me, then pulls back to admire me in the dress again. Her eyes are shimmery. Behind her, Dad's grinning his funny bottom-teeth-only grin. Quickly, I look down as if studying the sequins, scared to meet either of their gazes. I know we'll all get teary, and the last thing we need is some meltdown in the middle of the store and Mom telling the saleswoman her two-months-to-live sob story. We're a few towns away from ours, but it's Long Island—gossip travels fast.

Mom and Dad take the dress to the register while I pull on my jeans and hoodie. I look in the mirror. My mouth is smiling, but my eyes look faraway. I like the dress. I do. But I know if we had longer, we'd search every store until I found the perfect dress like the one I'd envisioned. We'd shop at Betsey Johnson, Jessica McClintock, Macy's, Bloomingdale's. I long not only for that other dress—the perfect one—but for the adventure of shopping with Mom, of looking high and low until we found it, and that moment of elation when we did.

I shake myself from the daydream. It can't be that way, and it's stupid to wish. *Stupid, stupid, stupid.*

On the drive home, Mom chirps on about all the accessories I'll need—shoes and a small purse and the right color nail polish. I make small sounds of agreement, but I'm not really listening. I'm somewhere else entirely, still back at the store, chilled by that moment when Mom pulled back to take me in. As if she was storing the snapshot for later. She and Dad stop at Boston Market to pick up chicken for dinner, and I stay in the car, staring at the dress hanging in plastic in the backseat. I keep rewinding that scene and watching it in slow motion, as my eyes fill with tears. Was that moment in the store the only time Mom will ever see me wear it?

Mom and Dad head back toward the car, laughing at something Dad said. Mom tilts her head back and cackles. "Billy!" Mom shouts, hitting him in the arm. I wipe away my tears and put on a happy face. Who knows how many more times like this we'll get?

Reality hits almost as soon as we get home. Dad's setting down the plastic bags of chicken and sides on the kitchen counter and Mom's shuffling through the mail. Red light flashes on the phone and everyone's busy, so I hit "play" on the answering machine.

"Hello. This message is for Sally. This is Irene from St. Luke's-Roosevelt. We have the results from your last blood test. Please call us back at 212-649-3425. Thank you."

Mom grabs the Boston Market receipt and a pen and scribbles down the number, looking down at the paper with a serious expression. Dad watches her, bushy eyebrows concerned. I bite my lip nervously. I get why they don't leave results on an answering machine, but I hate how they just leave all the options looming out there, because of course you assume it's the worst. With Stage 4 pancreatic cancer, chances are it *is* the worst. Mom smiles brightly at us, trying so hard, as if to say, "Don't worry! It was still a good day!" The energy in the room, the good stuff we all tried to hold onto from the store, seems to deflate.

Meanwhile, the answering machine beeps its annoying beep, signaling a second message.

"Hi Marisa! It's Laura, your favorite person in the world. C'mon you know it's true. Well, anyways, just calling to see how prom dress shopping was. Whoo! Prom! I can't wait. OK, well, I'm going to church and then to Aunt Mary's for dinner, but call me back after seven. Bye!"

It's almost embarrassing, the two messages side by side, one so serious and one so trivial. I smile at Mom, a serious smile, to show her I understand—to impart to her that it *was* a good day. Maybe that's all we can do between now and then, just try to have some good days. Hell, at this point, I'd even take some good seconds. Mom smiles back appreciatively, and it's like a small secret shared between us. We're miles away from where we used to be, but it's a tiny step back toward each other, and it feels good.

I eat dinner quickly, eager to go upstairs to my room to call Laura.

"Ohmygod, how was it? Did you get a dress? Is it maroon?"

Marisa / Sally

"It's silver. Well, pewter. Like a gun-metal gray," I explain, describing the dress we bought last week. I switch the receiver to my other ear.

"Oh good. And was it reasonable?" Sherry asks.

"This store always has good prices. We got Missy's prom dress there last year, too, when she went to Wilson's prom."

"She looked so pretty in the pictures. That rose color suited her fair skin."

"And you should see her now that she filled out a little. She looks like a princess."

"I'm sure she'll look even more beautiful this year."

She means it kindly, but her use of future tense—a future I won't live to see—silences me. Not knowing how to respond, I fidget with the clasp of my watch. From the day I learned I had cancer, I have not been able to take it off. I even sleep with it. Normally, I slipped the silver-and-gold band off my wrist right after *Seinfeld* ended at 11:30 p.m., but now it feels like I must keep track of time. I can't let it get away from me. I never felt that way before. I was much more carefree and naïve.

"I'm just glad I got to do this part with her," I ramble. "I always imagined prom dress shopping with Missy. It was so important to me, you know, all those mother-daughter rituals. But how will she do the rest without me…"

My voice gets hoarse and drops off entirely. Forever I've been dressing my daughter as a way to prepare her for life. The precious pink dress we carefully buttoned when she was a baby. The silver sequin belt that sparkled over her slinky black dress at the sixth-grade dance. The pearl-embroidered white gown custom-made for her bat mitzvah—the one we'd jokingly called a "mini wedding dress."

The thought gives me pause. Was there so much pressure on the prom dress because we all know the wedding dress will never happen?

"Sal, it's normal to feel scared," Sherry says.

She knows me so well. As my sister-in-law of more than forty years, Sherry is the closest thing I have to a sister. She met my older brother, Stuart, when she was only sixteen. Back in those days, relationships were very proper, so whenever she came to stay with us, she slept in my bed, tucked in tight with overcoats to prevent any "funny business" between her and Stuart. I was just happy to have an older girl to confide in, since I'd always been bullied by an older and a younger brother who teamed up against me. (Howie held my arms behind my back while Stuart punched me. It's hard to believe we're all close now as adults.) I picture Sherry on the other end of the phone, nervously twisting her phone cord and wiping silent tears from her eyes. I know how worried she is about me.

"Thanks, Sher," I say. "It's just…"

"What?"

"My work here is not *done*."

"I know, Sal."

"Everyone tells me to take it one day at a time, but there's so much left to do. Billy's so upset, and you know Jordan's not much of a student, and I told him he could take a semester off to spend time with me, but what if he does and then never goes back? And then Missy. She's so young, and there's graduation and prom…and she won't talk to me. She treats me like I'm already dead. Oh, Sherry, I just—I'm tearing apart my family. I can't stand the thought of missing all of this."

I started to cry in the middle and now I just keep crying. Poor Sherry. She just called to check in on me. I bet she wasn't expecting all this.

"Oh, Sal. It's OK to cry. You just have to take it one day at a time. Try taking a few deep breaths."

I do as she says. Inhale, exhale. I close my eyes. "I feel like I've been robbed."

"I know. I don't blame you," Sherry continues. "But you have such a strong spirit within you. Don't give up yet. Dr. Bruckner's right. A positive attitude *can* make a difference."

I whisk a pink tissue from the Kleenex box on my nightstand, surrounded by framed photos. Bill and me kissing in the '70s. Jordy and Missy as kids in matching pajamas. The four of us on vacation in Florida. *My family. I have to be strong for them.* I wipe my eyes.

"You're right, Sher," I say softly, pausing to blow my nose loudly. "I joined the Y today. I'm going to start swimming laps whenever I can."

"Good. Your family needs you healthy and strong for as long as possible. God won't take you until your work is done."

"I hope you're right," I pray, then hear a beep. "Oh, Sher, I'm getting call-waiting and it might be the nurse calling back with my blood test results. Can I give you a call tomorrow?"

"Of course. Of course."

I click the phone receiver. "Hello?"

"Hi, Sally! It's Laura. How are you feeling?"

"Laura!" I sing out. Her cheerful voice always perks me up. "I'm good, dear. How are *you?*"

"Good. I was actually just calling to tell Marisa that you guys should come visit me later at Nine West. I'm working 'til five. Boots are buy one get one half off, and there's a pair you'll like. They're *cute*, Sally. And Marisa needs prom shoes…"

"Oh! She told you about the dress. Good. Do you have anything silver?"

"I don't remember. We might. I'll look when I get in."

"Thanks, Laura." I lower my voice. "So, how's Missy doing?"

Laura stammers. "Um, she's fine, I think."

"I know it's a funny question to ask. Especially since she's downstairs in her room right now. I mean, I hear her. She's opening and closing her dresser drawers, the way she does when she can't decide what to wear. But every time I mention anything about me being sick, she just…she won't talk to me, Laura."

"I know," Laura says. "It's not you, Sally. She'll barely talk to *me* about it. I have to drag it out of her."

"Really? Even with you?" Missy usually tells Laura everything. I'm shocked.

"Yeah. It's really hard. Eventually she talks, though."

"OK. As long as she's talking to *someone*."

"Don't worry, Sally. I'll keep trying to get her to talk."

"Does she...does she cry?"

"Oh please, Sally. Marisa? Cry? She never even cried to me after breakups. Me, I cry over the littlest thing. Last week my brother teased me, and I ran to my room crying. My family thinks I'm crazy."

We laugh together, and it feels better to know I'm not alone in Missy's silence.

"I think Marisa maybe cries on her own time," Laura says gently.

"You're probably right," I agree. "Missy's lucky to have you. I'll go tell her you're on the phone, hang on."

"OK. Feel good, Sally! Maybe I'll see you later!"

"Thanks, dear." Her warmth bleeds through the phone and makes me miss Missy even more. She's always been right by my side. But now that I need her warm hugs and kisses more than ever, she's gone.

"Missy!" I call. "Laura's on the phone!"

She doesn't answer me, but I hear her pick up the phone. "Hi!" she squeals. I haven't heard her sound that happy in a while. Eavesdropping seems like a good idea, but I force myself to hang up. Missy needs her privacy. Especially now.

I put the receiver down softly, then pull out the small plastic tray beneath the phone that holds my speed-dial names. So many friends and relatives have reached out since they heard I was sick. Like my dear Aunt Ruthy, who has been a mother figure to me ever since my own mother died when I was forty, and who now calls weekly to check on me. My support system is unbelievable. If only I could catch up on phone tag. I look at the speed-dial numbers. The top three are standard: police, fire, ambulance. But even the so-called emergency numbers can't help me. I push the tray back in, pull it out again, push it in, pull it out.

One day at a time, Sherry had said. I picture strappy silver sandals to go with Missy's prom dress, and imagine a light-hearted trip together to visit Laura at Nine West. It's a simple wish, but it makes me smile. Dressing up is one of the many pleasures of having a daughter. Through the years, shopping has become an activity that brings us closer together. I still believe it has the power to do that, even now, when we feel so far apart.

I know what I have to do. I have to take a few more deep breaths. And I have to find a way to get Missy to talk to me.

CHAPTER 5
Blowup

Marisa / Sally

"Hang on," I say.
"Sure."

I turn up the volume. If this is the episode where Joey and Dawson finally make out, there's no way in hell I'm missing it for a phone call.

Although, it *is* Tony—and I kind of owe him after dodging his calls all last week. Wilson was home for spring break, and it just felt weird to talk to Tony. When Wilson is away, I feel sort of…single. I know that's so wrong. But when Wilson's home, it feels totally different. Suddenly he's calling every day, and we're hanging out after school, and going to see bands play shows on the weekends. He even came with me to visit my mom in the hospital for the first time. She goes for chemo every two to three weeks, and stays overnight for one night each time, and I felt guilty because I still hadn't been to visit her. I figured having Wilson with me would make me brave. Plus, I wanted him to see the reality of my new life. Maybe then he'd try harder to be there for me. My whole body shook as we took the

Long Island Rail Road to New York City, and then the subway to the hospital. I was terrified to walk into her room and see her looking sickly and sad. But when we arrived, she was sitting up in bed with her usual baseball cap on, making the nurses laugh and chatting normally with Dad. The most awkward part was Wilson. It was his first time visiting someone sick in the hospital, and he was so uncomfortable that he barely said a word as we ate takeout dinner from a deli down the block, balancing our paper plates on Mom's white hospital sheets. We were supposed to be there to cheer up Mom. Instead, Mom, Dad, and I spent the whole time trying to comfort Wilson, cracking weird jokes about the stale chicken cutlets that sat uneaten on our plates after resisting the efforts of our plastic cutlery. Still, I felt indebted to Wilson for coming and grateful when he held my hand the entire train ride home. It made me feel even guiltier about this weird pseudo-cheating with Tony. Nothing has actually *happened*, but now Wilson's back at school, and here I am, already an hour into my phone call with Tony.

"So what's the deal with Dawson and…uh, whatsaname? The neighbor chick."

"Joey," I say, faking a sigh. "Joey Potter. Have you learned *nothing* from our conversations?"

"I never even seen the show!"

"So?" I shoot back, secretly cringing at his poor grammar. "I told you there'd be a quiz."

"Nuh uh. Not another quiz. I think I failed the last one."

"You didn't fail. It was called 'Which nail polish are you?' And you're the one who wanted to take a *Seventeen* quiz! You know you secretly liked it."

"Oh yeah," he deadpans. "I loved every second."

"Anyway, Joey and Dawson," I say. "The deal is they're best friends."

"Time-out. I thought you don't talk to people during *Dawson's River*."

"*Creek*," I correct him. "And I don't. But ya know, sometimes I make exceptions…"

Even though I'd hung up on Wilson last week as soon as the theme song came on. Whatever. If he could keep up a conversation for more than twelve minutes, maybe I wouldn't have. Or if he had asked about my mom even once. Even though I avoid the topic with everyone else, for some reason I constantly feel furious with Wilson for not asking. Especially after he came with me to the hospital to see her, I really thought things would change. But he's just as silent on the topic as I am. Sometimes I just think that if I had that boyfriend who was my soulmate, I'd have one person who I could really share everything with, even the stuff about my mom—someone like Tony.

"Exceptions, huh?" he says now.

"Uh, yeah," I say, trying to switch gears from death to *Dawson's Creek*. "I swear if you watched just one episode, you'd like it."

"That's what all you girls say about every girly TV show."

"It's true," I insist, flopping stomach down onto my bed to face the TV, stretching the phone cord to its max from its spot on my nightstand. "So, Dawson realizes he's, like, in love with Joey, but she just thinks of him as a friend. So then he falls for the new girl in town, who's like, this blonde, slutty chick."

"Ooh, I like her already."

"Oh, quiet! Joey's *so* much better than her. She's smarter and nicer and prettier..." *And a flat-chested brunette*, I add silently, half defending my species, half needing Tony to choose Joey and, therefore, choose me.

"Ah! Fine. I'll like Joey."

I smile, satisfied, until the receiver clicks. The Mets game blares in the background. It's my dad in the den. *Click*.

"Uh, sorry, I think my dad picked up," I stammer, "but he hung up."

"So what's happening now?"

"Um, Dawson's best friend Pacey asked Joey to the homecoming dance."

"Oooh. That sounds scandalous."

Click. "Missy? I need to use the phone."

It's my dad, his voice gruff and annoyed. This is *so* embarrassing.

"Uh, OK Dad," I mumble, totally mortified. "Five minutes."

He hangs up.

"You gotta go?" Tony asks.

"No, no, it's fine…" I say, distracted. Tony is twenty—three years older than I am. He must think I'm such a baby. "So, um, Pacey. Yeah, he's in love with Joey, too. Basically, everyone's in love with Joey. She's the 'girl next door' or whatever."

"What does that even mean? No girls lived next door to me my whole life!"

I laugh. Maybe his grammar sucks, but he's really funny. Mom always says the most important quality in a guy is sense of humor…

Click. "Missy." The voice is angrier. "*NOW!*"

He hangs up.

"Dude, your dad sounds mad. You should go."

"But I have to finish telling you what happens," I stammer, even though I've missed most of the episode.

"OK, *sweethawt.*"

I burst out laughing. He always knows what to say to make me feel better.

"So Pacey shows up at homecoming with Joey, and Dawson gets *really* mad—"

Heavy footsteps pound up the stairs toward my room. *Shit.* I jump up from the bed, cradling the phone to my chest, as my dad busts open my door, red-faced and frighteningly mad.

"FINE!" Dad bellows, stomping toward me. "You won't get off the phone? Now you have NO phone! OK?! You've lost your phone privileges!"

"Dad, STOP!" I scream, covering the phone's mouthpiece with my hand. Did Tony hear all of that?

Bam! With one giant reach, Dad lunges at me, grabs the phone from my bony fist, and yanks it out of the phone jack.

"You have no respect for my privacy!" I scream, my voice shrill and my whole body shaking. "Give it back to me!"

Dad storms out of the room, holding my white phone captive. Shaking with rage, I chase him into the hallway, but he's already down the stairs.

"Give me back my phone!" I screech at him from the top of the stairs. The walls seem to shake and blur with my scream.

"At this rate, you're never getting it back!" Dad hollers, lunging toward me from the foot of the stairs. He glares at me and I'm shocked to see only fury in his eyes. It's the look he gives Jordan when they get into screaming matches. But I've always been his little girl. I'm about to scream back when a voice interrupts us.

"Billy, stop it!" Mom shrieks, seemingly out of nowhere.

Stunned, our heads swivel toward the upstairs landing. Mom's standing at the top step, scowling down at us, with messy hair and an oversize T-shirt. We hadn't even noticed she was there. She looks so fragile, but we're both too angry to stop.

"No!" Dad yells, eyes darting angrily from me to Mom. "She needs to be there for you and instead she's talking on the phone for three hours!"

"It was *not* three hours!" I yell back.

He glares at me, pure fury again, and I brace myself for what he says next.

"You're being selfish," he sneers, each word deliberate and slow. "Mom is sick, and this is how you act? I'm ashamed of you. I'm ashamed you're my daughter."

"Billy, don't *say* that," Mom yells.

"STOP IT!" I scream, squeezing my eyes shut and covering my ears. It's that wall-shuddering scream, and this time it's loud enough to make them both stop and stare at me, bewildered. I have the floor, but I have no idea what to say. I want to prove to them that I'm not the selfish girl they think I am. That I'm still the girl I used to be. "Beautiful inside and out," as my mom used to say. But I'm too hurt that they've stopped thinking of me that way. I'm too mad that they've abandoned me at the first sign of me being anything less than the do-gooder I've always been. I'm too worried that if they see me as bad, then that's who I'll become, and we'll all be broken forever.

"Do you want me to kill myself?" I try to yell, but my voice catches, and it comes out like a moan. "Is that what you want?"

"Missy, don't talk that way!" Mom shouts, her voice shrill. "Billy, look what you did, don't you see she's upset?"

Sobbing, I lean against the wallpaper and let my back slide down the wall until I'm sitting on the ground, knees up to my chin. I haven't cried since Mom was diagnosed, and now my throat can barely swallow against the tears and mucus and screams.

My parents continue bickering about who's being too hard on me (Dad) and who's letting me off too easy (Mom). Until they seem to realize they've gotten sidetracked from the person they're actually upset with: me. I'm still crying, partially because I don't really know what else to do, and I keep expecting Mom to come downstairs and comfort me, but instead she looks at me—hard. Ashamed, I stare at my knees, hugging them to my chest.

"I need to know if you're going to be there for me or not," Mom says in a deep, dead-serious voice that's even more frightening than Dad's roar.

The silence following the screams is eerie, and I realize they're waiting for an answer. A real answer from me. And I don't know what my answer is.

I look over at my brother's bedroom door. Lucky. I wish I were away at college like him, and didn't have to deal with this. But he *is* dealing with it. In fact, it's the first time in my life he's handling a situation better than I am. He's the one who looked devastated when she was diagnosed. He's the one who calls every day to see how she's feeling. I just can't *do* that. I know there has to be a bright part of the story. I know one day the doctors will call with results from the latest blood test and apologize profusely to my mother. "It was all a big mistake…a misdiagnosis. It's just a backache. Do some physical therapy and you'll be fine." We'll go out to Tofu, her favorite Chinese restaurant, to celebrate and laugh…

But as the weeks have passed, and my mom has grown weaker from chemo, it's painfully obvious: we'll never get that call. She'll never be magically cured. This will never go away. I feel childish for even making wishes; when will I realize there's no point? They don't come true. The reality seems even more blatant as I look at my dad, red-faced, my mom, sickly, both waiting for me to answer the question that's broken their hearts: *can I be there for her or not*? Their silence is heavy as I sit in the hall, crying, searching for my answer.

The truth is, only part of me believed the diagnosis was all a mistake. The other part killed her off entirely. In January the doctor said she had only two months to live. At that moment, for me, she died. It's already March, and if she won't be around much longer, why spend time with her now? Why bother? What's the point? I don't want to live to see how this ends. I know how it ends. It ends.

I stare at the bathroom across the hall. I'd heard of people using the shower rod. I'd considered it once before, a couple years ago, when my boyfriend, Jake, broke up with me. We'd dated all summer, but when the season ended, he decided we should, too. All my friends were dating his friends, and I was heartbroken to lose not only him, but entry into that exclusive group that had grown so close in just a few months. The day after he broke up with me, my parents went out shopping and my brother was at a friend's, and I was home alone. I decided to take a shower to calm down, and that's when I first noticed the shower rod. And the razor blade. But both were fleeting thoughts—a wish for an intense end to an intense romance. The ache to be as in love as Romeo and Juliet, the play we had read in English class—a love so strong it was more powerful than life. But I knew deep down we didn't have anything close to that. So instead I'd sat on the bathroom floor, naked, and sobbed. Later, I cracked apart a mix tape he'd made for me, the hard plastic leaving red welts on my fingers and hands.

But that was a stupid breakup. If only I were dumped right now instead of going through this. This awful thing that's too scary to even say out loud. This thing that terrifies me the most when I'm driving, especially if I'm first in line at a red light. Watching the cars pass before me is too tempting. Each SUV that swooshes by seems to egg me on, whispering, "Just take your foot off the break and hit the gas…"

In the moment, the thought of suicide feels powerful and real, and leaves me shaken as the light changes to green and I slowly make my way home. Hands trembling as I steer, I wonder why I didn't do it. I worry about the next time. But, by the time I pull into my driveway, I realize with great clarity: those moments don't come to hurt me, they come to save me. I've been trying to run away from it all, to avoid feeling the crushing collapse of my world. In those moments, it's as if my subconscious taps me on the shoulder and warns me: "Hey, you're not OK."

But that's all it is—a warning. As deep as my grief drags me down, my curiosity is an annoyingly bouyant balloon that lifts me back up. Despite everything, I still want to graduate, and go to prom, and go away to college, and get married, and see where the story of my life is meant to take me.

I replay the scene in my head. Did I really just tell my parents I might kill myself? I bury my face in my hands. The cry for help feels so stereotypical that I suddenly feel mortified for saying it out loud. Mostly, it's a way to avoid giving my mom an answer. Can I be there for her? Can I come home from school every day and walk up to her room? Ask her how she's feeling? Visit her in the hospital?

This is the first time in my life I can't just take the decent path. I've always been the good daughter. I've always done the right thing. But maybe deep down I'm as bad as they think I am.

"Missy," Mom says, still in that quiet, serious voice. "Just tell me, yes or no." I know the question breaks her heart.

I pause, take a deep breath, and wipe my nose with my sleeve. "I don't know if I can be."

It's the first time in months that I've been honest. But I thought honesty was supposed to feel good. Instead, my voice sounds small and weak. Mom blows her nose. Dad always teases her about her loud honk, but this time he doesn't say anything.

"I'll try," I say finally.

She reaches her arms toward me. I crawl up the tiled stairs and into her embrace, and she strokes my hair like I'm a little girl. So much of me wants to be that little girl again, when a good cry and a hug could cure anything. This hug feels uneasy, like there's still so much left unsaid, still so much work to be done to repair all that's broken. Mom's tears drip onto my scalp, but being this near to her freezes my own. I'm scared that if we have this crying moment together, it means I'll no longer be able to retreat—to my bedroom, to my private thoughts, to my escape route when I don't want to deal with it. My eyes dart around nervously looking for a way out, my nerves still programmed to *go, go, go*. I try to breathe through it. I'm just glad we're not in her room, where I'd be trapped. We're only on the landing.

Marisa / **Sally**

There. Now that she's in my arms, it'll be OK. I brush back her hair, damp where tears—mine and hers—have matted it.

"Missy…"

"Mmhmm," she murmurs into my oversize T-shirt.

"Do you want to see a therapist?"

She pulls away and looks at me, brown eyes flickering. Like

maybe I've turned on her.

"I just thought…it's hard for you to come to me. It's hard for you to talk to your friends, even though I know Laura cares for you a great deal. Maybe it'd be easier to talk to someone…not involved… who knows how to help."

Missy stays quiet. Just as she's coming back to me, of course I have to ruin it by suggesting therapy. What kind of mother am I?

"Maybe," she says timidly.

Oh, thank God. She doesn't hate me.

"You know, I didn't think I needed a therapist. But the first time I went for chemo, the hospital sent a social worker to talk to me. She sat in a chair near my bed and asked, 'Sally, do you feel depressed?' As soon as she said that, I started to cry."

"Really?" Missy asks, sounding surprised.

"Oh yeah," I say. "I told her, 'I have two kids and I just found out I have pancreatic cancer. Of course I'm depressed!'"

Missy bursts out laughing, and so do I. Then tears rush to her eyes and she starts crying again.

"Oh Missy," I say, hugging her. "Poor baby. You don't know how to feel."

"How…" she starts. "How do you find a therapist?"

I can't believe she's warming up to the idea. "Well, we would want to find one who's good with teens. Actually, when I saw that therapist through South Nassau hospital, he mentioned there was a female therapist there who specialized in cancer patients. I wanted to see her, but she couldn't see me because she only treats adolescents."

"Oh…"

"And South Nassau accepts our insurance." I search Missy's face for a sign that this is OK. She's acting nonchalant, but I can tell she's interested. It's the first time in weeks she's actually listening to me.

"Think about it. If you decide you want to try it, I can call to see if she has an opening." Was that too open-ended? Would she get

scared off and not follow through? "Many therapists have a full case load, so they don't always have room for new patients," I explain. There. That should get her going.

"Mom…?"

"Yes, doll?" Please let her say she wants me to call. I'll call right now. It's nearly 10 p.m., but I can at least leave a message. I'll say it's an emergency. I have cancer; this *is* an emergency. Then they'll have to call me back first thing tomorrow morning and maybe they can squeeze her in tomorrow afternoon. Missy can drive herself there after school. Or should I go with her? I think it might be best—

"I think I want to go to sleep," she says. Her brown eyes look so worn and old and sad. I've put a hole in her heart.

"Oh. OK, doll." I pause, then stammer awkwardly, "Can I have another hug?"

She hugs me again and lays in my arms for a moment. I don't want her to go. Once she leaves my embrace, walks down the stairs, and escapes into her room, I'm afraid she'll transform back into the hateful, silent girl who has stalked the house the past few weeks. But I have no choice; I have to let her go.

"Goodnight, Mom," she says.

"Goodnight, Miss."

CHAPTER 6

Therapy

Marisa / Sally

I'm a bad kid. One step into the therapist's waiting room teaches me that.

Three kids my age turn as the glass door slams behind me. I jerk at the noise. And their stares. Tossing her Manic Panic-dyed red hair, a pale girl eyes me, then returns to looking bored. Something shiny on one guy's chin reflects the afternoon sun, and I realize it's a labret piercing: a silver spear jutting out beneath his lower lip. A tall girl, slumped in her chair, eyes me up and down until she's positive that I feel like the biggest loser in the world. It's like I've entered a room full of misfits serving detention. But then again, I've never had a day of detention in my life, so what do I know?

I look down. My gray corduroys and black turtleneck sweater seem too preppy, even paired with thick-soled skater sneakers. Ever since Wilson introduced me to punk music last year, I've been testing out the look. But when I'm around kids like this, who seem like they were born with tattoos and piercings, I feel like a fraud. Now, at a freaking therapist's office, I feel it even more. Can they tell it's my first time?

Shaky-legged, I walk toward the reception desk. Fake nails twirl the phone chord. "The doctor's available Tuesday, April 13, at 2 orrrr…" she lingers, squinting at her appointment book, "Friday, April 16, at 8:30."

She looks up, finally, places a palm over the phone's mouthpiece, and raises her eyebrows like a question mark.

"I—" I begin.

"Friday at 8:30? Great. Let me just cancel your 5 o'clock today."

She scribbles in the book with purple pen. I look for a nail to bite. It's been my bad habit for seventeen years, but this is the shortest and rawest they've ever been. I gnaw on a cuticle.

"You're all set, Angela. See you Friday." She hangs up. I feel a sudden urge to run out the door and never return. "Can I help you?"

"I have an appointment? With Rosie O'Riordan?"

"What's your name?"

"Marisa…um, Bardach."

"Have a seat."

I choose a seat close to the receptionist and far from the other kids. Spinning the Blink-182 button on my messenger bag, I eye the door. *You can't leave*, I tell myself. *You have to try at least once. Besides, if you leave it means you have to go home sooner—to her.*

And home is still a shaky place, as if an earthquake hit and the threat of aftershocks loom each day. Ever since that terrible fight, an unspoken and cautious truce has settled among us. I feel it in the flicker of understanding in my dad's eye when he looks at me across the dinner table, and in my mom's eager smile when I come upstairs to greet her after school. Everything still feels a bit forced, a bit tense, but we all know we're trying. It's a solemn effort to be on our best behavior. Even if I still feel like the World's Worst Daughter, and even though I still sometimes long to run away from it all.

Oh well. I might as well do some homework while I'm waiting. I pull out my Spanish worksheet. *Write a dialogue between two strangers*. Ha. So many choices. A first-time patient and a therapist?

A prepster and a goth girl? A face-pierced freak and...

The door next to the reception desk opens, revealing a woman in a navy-blue cardigan set and a girl my age. "See you next week," the woman says as the girl leaves the office. The woman looks over at me. "Marisa?"

Shit.

I smile at her. I can't help it. A big grin on my face is normal for me, or at least it used to be. I'm still not used to all this seriousness and sadness. But then I worry that smiling is weird here and quickly put on a solemn expression. Jumping up, I cram my worksheet into my bag and haul it onto my shoulder. *Crap.* My cuticle is bleeding. I press my finger against my pants to hide it.

"I'm Rosie," the woman says, holding open the door for me. My mom had called her, explained the circumstances, and set up the appointment. All I had to do was show up. It didn't sound like much, but as we walk down the white corridor, I glance back at the waiting room. Still time to make a run for it...

"It's just a left here, a right, and then another right at the end of the hall," she directs me.

Her office is small and undecorated. A desk, her chair on wheels, two stationary chairs for her patients. I eye the two chairs suspiciously. I imagine the other chair is for when you're really bad and she makes one of your parents come in. I cringe at the thought and drop my stuff in that chair, squashing the mental image of my mom sitting there crying or my dad glaring with a disapproving look on his face. I slump into the other chair. Straighten my posture. Fold my hands in my lap. Unfold them. Look at my cuticle. It's stopped bleeding. At least for now.

Rosie closes the door, sits at her desk, and looks around. What is she searching for so intently?

Suddenly, she reaches into her file cabinet and places a box of Kleenex on the edge of her desk, closest to me.

So that's what she thinks? That I'm going to come in here like every other patient and blubber in her office? Fuck that. Fuck her. I vow to never, ever cry in front of her.

"So usually on the first appointment, we start by gathering some information," she says, opening a manila folder and placing a few forms and a pen in front of me. Her periwinkle blue eyes twinkle, as if she's revealing that we're going to bake cookies. "You can go ahead and fill those out, and then we'll continue."

When I'm done, I slide the completed forms across the table. She glances at my answers, nodding her head every so often, as if saying, "As I suspected." *Great*, I think, *I'm typical.*

"Well, Marisa," she says, looking up and smiling at me. It's a smile of sympathy and enthusiasm. A smile I imagine she has perfected over the years. She probably gives this smile to every patient, a million times a day. "I'd like to ask you some more questions about yourself, if that's all right with you."

"Sure."

"Have you ever seen a social worker before?" She pauses, pen in hand, notepad on desk.

"No." She scribbles that down. Hang on a second. I thought she was a therapist. She's a social worker?

"Well, I'm a licensed social worker," she begins, pointing to the framed diploma hanging above her desk. The calligraphy is so fancy that the Rs in her name don't even look like Rs, more like a swirly maze. "I help patients and their families cope with difficult situations and provide a safe space for you to talk. I'm affiliated with South Nassau hospital, and I specialize in helping cancer patients, which is how your mother found me. But everything you say here is said in confidence, according to the doctor-patient code of confidentiality. The only circumstance under which I would contact your parent or guardian is if I'm concerned that you might cause harm to yourself—if you appeared to be having suicidal thoughts."

I nod solemnly. I was such a good girl before all this. Now I'm trying to convince a doctor I'm not having suicidal thoughts. Even though I sort of am. Well, mostly that one time…does that count?

"Do you have any history of depression?"

"Umm…" I hesitate, unsure. Memories flash through my mind. Grandpa dying sophomore year. Grandma dying junior year. Talking on the phone to my cousin Susi, telling her I didn't think I believed in God anymore—how could He let people we love die? The breakup with Jake and crushing the mix tape he gave me, watching through blurry tears as the plastic edges scraped my hands. Finding out Mom had cancer and barely reacting, except to decide every day in my car that I shouldn't drive into the water, into oncoming traffic, through the display windows of the Gap…

"It's OK if you're unsure," Rosie says kindly. "Have you or anyone in your family been diagnosed as clinically depressed?"

"No," I say, thankful that Mom and I talked about this last night. Mom explained that what I'm feeling is probably "situational depression," since it's tied to her illness, and that this is different from "clinical depression," a chemical imbalance where you're prone to feeling sad and there might not even be a reason why. Clinical's what Tony told me he has the other night. I was so upset to hear it, even though I'd sort of guessed. Several times at band practice he'd blown up at the guitarist or bassist, then stormed out. He'd return five or ten minutes later, his eyes red from crying. Sometimes there'd be an apology; sometimes we'd just silently resume playing. The guys all seemed used to it and easily forgave his outbursts. I just sort of watched, and tried to give him a small smile when he returned. *I'm sad all the time, too*, I longed to tell him. Maybe that's why I felt I could one day confide in him about my own sadness or depression, or whatever the hell Rosie wants to label it.

"Have you ever felt depressed before? Meaning, more than what you would consider your typical level of sadness or anger?"

"I guess…?"

"When did you feel that way?"

"Um, well, my grandpa died two years ago. And my grandma

died last year. They lived in Florida, but I was, um, really close with them. So, um, yeah." She scribbles that down.

"Any other times?"

"Well, two summers ago, I guess. When my boyfriend dumped me."

"During these times, did you ever have thoughts of suicide?"

"Um, once...after he dumped me. But I never, um, did anything." Are we even going to talk about my mom? I thought that's why I was here. She scribbles for even longer.

"Are you currently taking any medications?"

"Um, yeah, birth control...because my period's really irregular." This is so embarrassing! Why does she have to know this? She writes it down. Ugh!

"Do you drink?"

I think back to Hailee's parents' holiday party, where we smuggled spiked punch into her tiny bathroom and each took sips. And a few weekends ago at a friend's house, when Tony and I shoved Fruit Loops into our cans of beer and tried to fish them out with our tongues. Then I think about the popular kids who probably drink every weekend.

"No."

"Never?"

"A couple times. But just a little."

"Smoke cigarettes?"

"No."

She raises her eyebrows.

"I swear! Never."

"Do you take any drugs?"

"No!" I'm so surprised by the question that I half-shout my answer. She raises her eyebrows again. "I'm really just kind of a Goody Two-shoes."

It's the first time I feel like I have to convince someone of who I am, at a time when *I'm* not even really sure who I am.

"How about your family? Who do you live with?"

"Um, my mom and dad. And my brother, sometimes—he's in college."

"What is your brother's name?"

"Jordan." She scribbles that down.

"How old is he?"

"Twenty. Three years older than me."

"Where does he go to school?"

"URI...um, in Rhode Island."

"Do you have a boyfriend?"

"Yes," I giggle nervously. Is she going to ask if we've had sex? Oh God, I hope she doesn't. I mean, we haven't—we're both still virgins—but we're each other's "first" lots of things. First serious relationship, first "I love you," first, well, other stuff...

"What's his name?"

"Wilson."

"Does Wilson go to school with you?"

"No. Not anymore. He's a year older than me so he graduated. Now he goes to college in Pittsburgh. So it's long distance."

"That's far away," she remarks.

"Yeah. We talk online. And see each other on breaks."

"How about friends? Who are your closest friends?"

"Laura. And Hailee and Shari—but not as much anymore. Mostly Laura." More scribbling.

"What year are you in?"

"Senior."

"Oh, wow. That's a big year."

"Yeah." I think of prom and smile.

"You seem excited about senior year," she observes.

Shit. I forgot I'm not supposed to smile here. "Oh, well, yeah. Some of it."

"Do you like school?"

"Yeah."

"What are your favorite subjects?"

"English. And Spanish."

"Do you do well in school?"

"Yeah," I blush, then blurt out, "I'm one of those dorky honor roll kids."

"Oh, that's wonderful. You should be proud."

I blush again and look down.

"What are your plans for after graduation?"

"Um, college, I guess? To study, like, writing and communication? But I'm not sure where."

"Have you heard from any schools yet?'

"Well, I got into Binghamton and Penn State, but I don't really want to go to either one. BU, um, Boston University, but it's too expensive," I say, ticking them off one by one on my fingers. "And I just got into Syracuse. Into Newhouse? Their communications school? It's one of the top three in the country, and they gave me a $10,000 scholarship."

"Wonderful!" she says, with a radiant smile. My mom had thrown her arms around me after I'd ripped open the envelope and we saw the acceptance letter and scholarship award. All that week I'd over-heard her calling all her friends to say I'd won a "merit scholarship," so proud that I'd earned it all on my own. She was generous not to admit how many nights she'd stayed up with me throughout high school, reading in my room just to keep me company while I'd stressed over studying for a test or writing the last few pages of a paper.

"Thanks," I say shyly. "The only one I'm waiting to hear back from is Cornell."

"Those are all terrific schools," she marvels. "How about outside of school? Do you participate in after-school activities?"

"I'm in Model Congress…Yearbook committee…and I play drums in a band."

"Drums—wow!" she says. And scribbles.

"So, Marisa, if you wouldn't mind, I'd like to hear your opinion of why you're here and what you hope to get out of our sessions together." She looks up at me expectantly.

"Oh, OK. Well, my mom has, um, a tumor…in her pancreas. Cancer, I guess. She's going for chemo. At St. Luke's-Roosevelt? In the city? I guess I just want to figure out how to deal with it all. My mom and dad are mad at me for not being there for them. And I'm supposed to go away to college…"

"Well, I certainly hope I can help you through some of this. I'm sure it's all been very overwhelming. Do you know what stage the cancer is at?"

"Stage 4." It's one of the few stats I'd overheard that I could remember.

"Do you know what that means?"

"Not really."

"The stages are 1 through 4," she begins. "Stage 1 is when the tumor is isolated in an area that's easy to remove or treat. Stage 4 means it has traveled to another organ and is less easy to remove or treat. Do you know if the doctors found any tumors aside from in the pancreas?"

"Liver?"

She winces ever so slightly. "Once a cancer spreads, that does mean it's harder to treat."

"Oh."

"Did the doctor give your mother a prognosis?"

"Well, the first doctor said she had two months to live. But her new doctor says he's kept people alive for up to ten years. I dunno, it's April, already three months since she was diagnosed, so I guess the two months thing was wrong. I don't really know what to believe."

"It's so hard to know, but it sounds like she has an excellent doctor. And they make so many strides in cancer research every day."

"Yeah." It's nice to hear optimism from a stranger who actually knows about cancer, but I still feel like my mom is on borrowed time. Like two months was the real diagnosis and anything extra is just dumb luck and won't last.

"How about symptoms? Is she tired or nauseous? Is she losing her hair?"

"Um, all three, I guess. She says she wakes up and finds clumps of hair on her pillow. It hasn't all fallen out, but it's pretty thin. She wears a hat most of the time, and my dad's taking her to get a wig today." I picture Mom's little face, childlike and vulnerable without her usual dark bangs and shoulder-length wisps. Her new look was so disarming, it made my eyes fill.

"We talked a little bit before about depression. Would you consider yourself depressed now?" Rosie's blue eyes study me intently.

I think back to the drive here. The way the red lights taunt me to plunge my car into oncoming traffic. In my head I hear the satisfying crunch of metal on metal, the sigh of relief as the chaos fades to black. I feel so numb in those moments. I don't think I'd really do it, but what if one day the numbness takes over?

"I think so?" I say quietly, questioning.

She nods, looking up at the clock. "Well, our time is up for today. I'd like to recommend we meet once a week. How does that sound?"

"Good! Sure!" I say, too fast, too enthusiastically. Is it really over? All she had found out was my brother's name and my favorite subject at school. I congratulate myself for tricking her, just like Matt Damon fooled Robin Williams in *Good Will Hunting*. As much as I want to get better—to regain my closeness with my parents, to fill the gaping hollowness I feel inside—my reflex is still to hide all my feelings away.

"I know this session was mostly taking inventory," she says, as if reading my mind. "Next week we'll be able to talk more in-depth."

Crap. I picture Matt Damon crying in Robin Williams's arms, and vow again not to let my guard down in front of her.

"I'll come walk you out," she says, standing and opening the door so I can exit.

"Thanks." I grin, then stop myself. I really need to control my facial expressions.

The path through the hallway still seems completely unfamiliar. I let Rosie call out navigation signals behind me. Finally, we reach the door to the waiting room.

"It's just this way," she says. "I hope to see you next week."

The "hope" part makes me realize it's optional. I bet lots of people ditch out after the first visit. Maybe I would, too. "OK, bye. Thank you!"

"Take care," she says.

I dig my keys out of my messenger bag and walk toward my car. I plan to take the long route home. I need time to think.

Marisa / **Sally**

Don't think so much that you forget to swim, I scold myself. But fifteen laps into swimming at the YMCA's indoor pool, I still can't get this thought out of my head: why do bald men try so hard to cover up the fact that they're bald? It's especially hard to ignore given that the geriatric gentlemen who share the lanes with me don't have much left on top. Trust me: I've seen them minus their swim caps.

I pause at the end of the lane to adjust my own swim cap and goggles. Aquatic exercise is new to me. I had begun swimming laps a few weeks earlier—upon the hospital social worker's suggestion that it might calm me—but I still fear the lifeguard might suddenly toot his whistle and accuse me of being an imposter. I look up at the young lifeguard now, but he's gazing out the window. So much for safety. I kick off the side of the pool and begin the breaststroke, catching a quick glimpse of another better-off-bald comb-over man wrapping a towel around his waist before heading off to the locker room. *Just shave it!* I fight back yelling.

Seriously. The comb-over, the spray dye on the bald spot, the unsightly toupee that everyone knows is just that. Why do men bother?

Bald is not a bad look for a man. As a matter of fact, it can be quite attractive. Remember Yul Brynner, the Russian actor in *The King and I*? And nowadays so many young men and actors shave their heads just to achieve that bald look. It can be very sexy.

Whoops. Here I am, thinking so much about sexy bald men that I've started to swim diagonally. I nearly bump right into Baldy himself! I need to focus during the backstroke, or I'll really be a goner. Why didn't anyone tell me swimming is more dangerous than chemo? This guy looks terrified.

He'd be even more frightened if he saw *me* without my swim cap. Bald for a woman is definitely *not* a good look, I'd decided. Only if you're between the ages of eighteen and maybe thirty and have model-perfect features is it attractive. But a fifty-seven-year-old woman bald from chemotherapy and in the grips of a deadly can-cer—this was definitely not an attractive sight. No matter how sexy the swimsuit.

As I finish my final crawl stroke, I realize my current hairdo bears a striking resemblance to Bill's comb-over—the style he wore for the first fourteen years of our marriage. Now I understand his discomfort. A few pathetic, long strands hang from the base of my skull to my shoulder blades, but I refuse to cut them. After all, it almost resembles a normal hairdo when I wear one of my now-trademark Gap baseball caps (color coordinated to match my outfits, of course).

I think of the summer Bill finally cut his comb-over. The kids were at sleep-away camp, and we'd been empty nesters for a month, escaping for blissful long weekends to bed-and-breakfasts in Balti-more and Maine. In a moment of boldness, Bill bravely cut that dreadful comb-over. When the kids saw him on visiting day, they did a double take. "Doesn't he look handsome?" I'd boasted.

Now would be the time for Bill to tease me. After all, I've been teasing him about his baldness since we met. *Hit me with your best shot*, I long to egg him on. But Bill is too much of a gentleman to get me back. In fact, out of sympathy and empathy, he's taking me wig shopping today. What a *mensch*.

I rest at the end of the lane for a few minutes to catch my breath. Having been born under the Pisces sign, I love swimming. Thank God that hospital social worker recommended it. It already feels like it's working. With every lap, I can feel how strong my body is and how able to fight this disease.

Even if I am bald.

Walking into the locker room, practically blind without my glasses, I'm shocked to see an elderly gentleman with a towel wrapped around his bottom half. He looks just as appalled to see me.

"Are you in the wrong place or am I?" I ask, laughing.

"I think you are, my dear," he chuckles, as another man—this one without a towel—walks past us.

I scurry out, pausing only to look behind me as the door shuts. Yep, definitely the sign for men's room. I'd blame chemo brain, but I've done this for years, often only realizing my error when I see the urinals. I'm still giggling as I walk into the women's room.

I shower and pull on my jeans and striped shirt and baseball cap, trying to hide my naked body and balding head. When I exit the gym at 5 p.m., Bill's car is right out front, waiting to pick me up.

I relay my locker-room mishap, and his eyebrows shoot up. "Sally!" he laughs. It's actually a cheerful twenty-minute drive to the wig shop in Cedarhurst, surprising us both.

However, a hush falls over us as we step carefully into the upscale wig shop. We chose the store because it specializes in more natural-looking human hair rather than synthetic wigs. In fact, the store's main clientele are the Orthodox and Hasidic population in Long Island's Five Towns. Married women in those sects of Judaism wear wigs for modesty, covering their natural hair the same way other women won't leave the house without a bra. My reason for being here feels so different, though I suppose it's a type of modesty I crave, too—one that lets me not be singled out for being sick.

"Hello, gorgeous!" The shop owner interrupts my thoughts, emerging from the back and ushering us warmly into the store. "I am Rodolfo," he announces in a flamboyant voice, thick with an indistinguishable foreign accent (maybe South American?) that makes him sound like a stylist to the stars.

Rodolfo leads us around the store, his thick, lustrous locks bouncing off his shoulders, and I immediately feel the twinge of hair envy that's only worsened as I've lost mine. I gaze up at a tall bookshelf featuring dozens of Styrofoam heads jauntily wearing wigs—from Farrah Fawcett's feathered mane to a spikey biker chick 'do. Which wig would I wear? Would any flow as beautifully as his hair, or even fall flat like mine? To the left of the bookcase, a few plush barbershop chairs face a mirrored wall. Rodolfo explains that's where women get their wigs serviced, as if we're just coming in for a simple shampoo, cut, and blowout. I wonder who we're fooling. Ourselves?

As I show Rodolfo photographs of precancer Sally—a big smile and wispy brown hair falling in layers to my shoulders—and take off my hat to reveal my measly remaining strands, I'm relieved Bill and I decided to come alone on our first visit. We worried it might upset Missy, and, besides, she's at her first therapy appointment today. I pray it's going well.

When we get home that night, Missy glosses over the therapy appointment, though I'm happy when she says the woman is nice and that she felt comfortable. What she really wants to talk about is the wig. I try to describe the wig they're creating for me as best as I can. But when she comes to pick it up with us a few weeks later, I can tell she's taken aback—that she expected the wig to look like my old hair. Though who would want that? Thin, flyaway, and stick straight even when I tried everything (a pick, hair spray) to give it even a smidge of body.

This wig is certainly *not* my old hair, Missy and I agree as I model it for her in the store. It is my new and improved hair. The tresses I'd envied on other women. The full, luxurious mane I'd longed for my whole life: chestnut-brown locks falling in long layers a few inches below my shoulders with a thin curtain of bangs that always behave. I'd gotten the hair of my dreams, but the price I'd paid was an incurable cancer. A harsh lesson in vanity, for sure.

CHAPTER 7

Opening Up

Marisa / Sally

"How was therapy?" That's Laura's first question after picking up on the first ring. What ever happened to hi?

"Um, it was OK, I think," I stammer.

"Did you lie down on a couch?"

"No," I laugh, relieved it's over and that I actually know the answers to questions like these. Truth is, I always wondered what therapy was like.

"Were you sitting in a chair?"

I sigh, knowing Laura's usual line of questioning means I should just tell the whole story from the beginning. To Laura, it isn't a good conversation unless it lasts over an hour and causes our parents to yell at us to stop hogging the line.

"No, I was sitting on a waterbed," I joke. "Yes I was sitting in a chair! And so was she."

"Was she nice?"

"Um, yeah. She seemed nice."

"How old was she?"

"I'm so bad with age…I dunno. Forty-ish?"

"OK, that's good, that's good," she says. I can picture her nodding, her eyebrows scrunched and serious. "It means she's experienced."

"Yeah, and she actually knows a lot about like, cancer, and all the medical terms."

"Oh, wow! That's great, Maris!"

"Yeah," I say, rolling my eyes at her enthusiasm. "Of course that also means she knows how to translate the medical BS into stats that are totally scary."

"Really?" Laura draws in her breath like a mini-gasp. *Drama queen*, I think to myself, not wanting to admit that it scared me, too. Her voice falls to a hush. "What did she say?"

"Well, there are, like, stages in cancer. The doctor said my mom has Stage 4, and I sort of knew what that meant, but not really. And she basically said it's like the worst kind you could have."

"Whyyy?" Laura asks. Worry stretches the word to a wail.

"Well, it was in the pancreas, but it's already spread to the liver. So it's harder to treat." I lean back against my pillows, proud of my newfound knowledge. Then I remind myself how disturbing it is that at seventeen I can recite facts about Stage 4 cancer.

"Are you going to go back to her?"

"Yeah. Once a week."

"That's good!" There's that cheerleader voice again. If I tell her I failed my last Calc test (which I did), she'll probably still say, "That's good!" Actually, she won't. She's so good at Calc and can't understand why I don't love it. Love it? Sometimes I don't understand how we're best friends.

"So what's going on with James? Did he call you?" Now that I've switched to her crush, I'm sure she'll change the subject.

"Oh, you don't want to hear about that," she says. "With every-thing with your mom…" she trails off. I remember why we're best friends: she's seriously the nicest person in the world.

"Laura! You have to tell me!" I say, laughing. "I'm your best friend—hello?!"

"Well, then I have a story for you," she says. I imagine her smiling.

"No!" I shout. "What happened?"

"He called me last night and was like, 'What's up?' I said, 'Not much. What's up with you?'"

This is what I mean about Laura liking hour-long conversations. But she did listen to everything about my therapist appointment. I try to be patient. Why is it that I'm always looking for an excuse to hang up with Laura, but I can spend three hours on the phone with Tony? He came over after school a few days ago to watch our favorite movie, *The Wedding Singer*. Mom and Dad were at the hospital, so we had the house to ourselves. Laughing side by side on the couch, I liked to think I was the adorable Drew Barrymore, and Tony was the silly, singing Adam Sandler who falls in love with her. The only piece that doesn't add up is Wilson—he isn't "Glenn," Drew's sleazy fiancé who cheats on her. Wilson has a good heart: he made me a paper shoe when I lost my flip-flop in a mosh pit last summer, hugged me so hard he lifted me straight off the ground when I visited him at college last semester, and just last night he IM'ed me "I miss you, Tubby"—his ironic nickname for me that was funnier when I was skinnier. Recently I've started to worry that I *am* getting tubby, as my junk food binges begin to show in my too-tight jeans, my once-flat belly now spilling over the waistband when I sit down. But I know Wilson only says it affectionately, to show he loves me in his own weird way. Besides, he has no idea I've put on weight. Even with Laura, I just claim it's bloating from my birth control, too embarrassed to admit that overeating is the only way to numb the noise in my head. No, Wilson isn't Glenn. But something in Drew's unhappiness, when she tries on her wedding dress and pretends to marry Adam Sandler instead of Glenn, echoes in my heart.

"So he was saying he hung out with Brendan," Laura continues. Uh-oh. I think I missed a big chunk of the story. I better try to catch up. "And Brendan asked him, 'What's going on with Laura?' which I thought was a good sign because boys don't usually ask their friends about girls, ya know?"

"Yeah—so what did he tell him?" I ask.

"He said, 'We're just hanging out.' Which I guess is OK, because I mean, it's not like we're boyfriend and girlfriend, we only hung out that one time and even though it was a Saturday night it was with all his friends so I don't think it really counts as a date, do you?"

Her sentence is so long I have to say it again in my head.

"Umm..." I begin.

"And anyway I have a lot going on with Sportnite coming up and you and I have to learn our dance routine, and then prom and who even knows if he'd be a good prom date. I mean, I don't even know if he likes to dance, and you know me, Marisa, I am going to be shaking my booty on the dance floor so I gotta find someone who's gonna *dance!*"

I laugh. Even at "a mile a minute," as my mom says, Laura can really crack me up. Besides, just last week I was complaining to Laura about my own prom drama. Wilson had griped on the phone yet again about coming to prom, and I had shot back, "Fine, maybe I'll just take Tony instead." Sulkily, but in a quiet, firm voice he had said, "No, I'll go." I had gotten my way...I think. Part of me wanted him not to go; part of me wanted to take Tony. I didn't say that part to Laura. She's never understood what I see in Wilson, and bugs me all the time that Tony's in love with me. With her, I just stick to my alibi: Tony knows I have a boyfriend. The only person who seems to understand is my cousin Susi, who says maybe you can love different people in different ways, and that makes me feel better.

I turn my attention back to Laura. "Do you think you'll see James this weekend?"

"I don't know. He didn't bring it up and I was like no way in hell am I gonna bring it up. That's, like, *his* job, ya know?"

"Yeah," I say, even though I disagree—I actually think it's cool for girls to make the first move—but I know old-school Laura will never go for this. There's a rare pause in the conversation, and, worried she'll want to talk more about therapy and cancer, I make my exit.

"Anyway, I should probably go set the table. Ya know, this whole 'trying to be a helpful daughter' thing."

"That's good, Maris." There's that line again. "Your mom would like that."

"Yeah," I agree, knowing she's right and knowing that I still really don't want to do the right thing.

"OK, well call me after dinner," she says. One phone call a night is never enough for her. I used to feel the same way about Laura, until my mom got sick. Now I'm afraid every conversation might suddenly veer off into unchartered territory. A place I can't go yet—not with my best friend, not with my boyfriend, not with a therapist, not with anyone. Laura must sense this because she suggests something light. "We'll catch up on *Felicity.*"

"Sounds good," I say, thinking a TV recap sounds safe enough. "Bye!"

"Bye!"

Marisa / Sally

Overhearing Missy giggling on the phone with Laura reminds me of my own girlfriends, who I've neglected a bit over the past few weeks. Tired from chemo and admittedly a little depressed by this sudden and scary shift in my life, picking up the phone just hasn't seemed that appealing.

Even now, lounging in bed while the tangy scent of Bill's barbecue chicken wafts upstairs, I can't bring myself to call back my friend Rona. We used to talk daily, and while Bill liked to heckle us that all we talked about was our periods, there was something comforting about chatting with a fellow mom about the banalities of everyday life. Now it all seems so trivial. What would we even talk about?

Cancer is not exactly the easiest segue to other, lighter topics.

Judging from the giggles tinkling up the stairs from her bedroom, Missy's still able to have those lighter conversations. Therapy has seemed to help her open up a bit more, at least with Laura, if not yet with me.

And her thoughts on friendship have certainly come a long way from when she was a little girl.

I remember years ago, after a long phone call with Rona, Missy, who was nine or so, came to my room.

"Mommy, why do you talk to Rona so much?" she demanded, hands on hips.

"What do you mean?" I asked, taken aback by her tone and trying to figure out what had upset her.

"You're supposed to just talk to Daddy," she said boldly.

I laughed in surprise. So young and already trying to wrap her mind around the intricacies of friendship and marriage.

"Well, Missy, I love Daddy and we talk to each other all the time. But you can't talk to your husband about *everything*. That's what girlfriends are for!"

Missy thought this over. I could tell she still wasn't convinced that I wasn't somehow cheating on Bill by having friends. Oh boy.

"That's why I always tell you to choose nice girlfriends," I continued. "Female friendships can sometimes be catty and cruel, but if you find good and true girlfriends, those friendships can last a lifetime."

Missy's brow unfurled. She seemed to understand.

Reluctantly, I get out of bed to use the bathroom before dinner. All those years ago, I hoped I was imparting a life lesson to Missy on friendship and marriage, and the difference between. But now— adjusting my gray terrycloth turban in the mirror—I realize that since I've become sick, my own lines have begun to blur. Sure, I'm still keeping in touch with my friends: with Rona, and Sherry, and my college roommate Bonnie. But Bill has become my everything.

Marriage isn't perfect—so my psychiatrist told me back in the day when all I did was idealize it. That's what happens when you're thirty and still not married. But now, after twenty-two years of marriage (I married Bill at thirty-four), I've discovered for myself that marriage has its ups and downs. But then there's love beween a man and woman—I'm not just talking about romantic love or sexual love, but faithful, generous, forgiving, liking and loving love. That's what I have with my Billy.

So my dream did come true. He has my utmost respect and friendship. He has my undying love. But most of all, he has given me so much emotional respect and love and support. Without him I could never get through this cancer. The way he's cared for me and about me and admired me and respected me.

But, most of all, we've always been able to love our children and raise them with love and we've always been able to laugh together. That laughter has always been the glue that's kept us together, not only as a couple but as a family—we all have a good sense of humor. It's the only way to get through life.

"Do things earlier than I did," I often joke to Missy when we talk about marriage and children. She laughs back, insisting I'm the only mom who's encouraging teen pregnancy just because I want a grandchild. It's a running joke, but I'm half-serious. It's been the happiest part of my life. I want her to have more time to enjoy it while she's young—and healthy. I think she knows I'm kidding, that it's more important to find the right person than to find him right now. But sometimes she seems so intent on forcing a relationship to work, even if it's not quite right, that I worry I've taken it too far.

"Chicken's on!" Bill calls upstairs to us, and I feel my worry lift a bit. A homecooked meal with my devoted husband and slowly-coming-around daughter. Maybe the banalities of life are still worth celebrating, perhaps even more so now.

CHAPTER 8
College Decision

Marisa / Sally

"An envelope came today—from Cornell," Mom says when I get home from school.

Big or small? Big or small?

She holds it up.

Small.

She hands it to me.

Here goes nothing…

We walk toward the kitchen table where I open it, scan it, then read it aloud in my snootiest Ivy League accent:

"Dear Ms. Bardach,

We regret to inform you that you have been waitlisted for Cornell University's College of Agriculture and Life Sciences. As space becomes available, we will review applicants to make additional admissions offers. You can expect to hear from us no later than May 31."

Mom looks at me expectantly.

I feel like crying. I'm smart—why didn't I get in?

She looks harder.

I don't want to wait until May to find out. I just want to know where I'm going to school. Laura's going to Hofstra and Shari's going to Penn State. When my friends and Aunt Sherry and Mr. Minor ask me, I just want to say...

"I'm going to Syracuse!" I yell out, surprising even myself.

"Really?" she asks.

"Yeah!"

"REALLY??" she asks again, louder.

"Yeah..."

I look at her face. Is it OK? Is she OK?

"Missy!!!" She screams, and I scream, and we jump up and down and hug each other.

After months of bad news, the good news is exhilarating. And Mom's excitement makes me feel like we're back on the same team. We started this process together, way before she got sick, with Mom encouraging me to consider a growing field called media and communications and researching schools within a five-hour radius of Long Island. Together we flipped through college brochures and websites, oohing and aahing over creative majors like advertising and magazine journalism and glossy photos of ivy-covered buildings and grassy quads. I've always loved writing, and so does my mom, but neither of us knew it could be a real career until then.

"Newhouse," Mom says now with a dreamy sigh, as we smile at one another.

And then the reality of it zooms into focus, and my fears flash by like a montage. Me, alone, five hours from home. Me, alone, hearing about bad blood test results. Me, alone, clutching the phone while Dad says, "She's gone, Missy, she's gone." Me, alone, regretting for the rest of my life that I wasn't with her at that final moment, that I was a bad daughter up until the very end.

I look at Mom and burst into tears.

Marisa / <u>Sally</u>

I grab her and hold her, my poor Missy who never cries this way— so suddenly, so openly.

"I don't even want to go to college," she sobs. "I don't want to leave you when you're sick."

Shushing her fears, I ease her into her chair at the kitchen table and pull my chair close to hers so our knees are touching.

"Now I know what Jordan feels like," she says miserably, tears still falling.

I try not to cry, but I can't control it. My little girl, the happiest and most well-adjusted person I know, and I've broken her heart.

"I'm so sorry to have done this to you," I weep. "You must hate me."

She stops crying and looks me in the eye.

"Mom, I don't hate you," she says firmly, grabbing my hands in hers. "I've never hated you, and I don't blame you."

The words I've been praying to hear for so long. I can tell she means it, and that the therapist really is helping her adjust to this terrible new reality. But I know in my heart that despite all the years I tried to protect her and Jordan, and despite the fact that I didn't wish this on myself, I've hurt the two people—three including Bill— whom I love the most. And for this, even though I know I'm the victim of cancer and so are they, I still hate myself.

"I wish I knew that there was a finite period of time when I'd be over this and in remission," I tell her, taking a deep breath. "But I don't know that. I do know that I am not dying now, and I want you to go away to school because it's one of the best experiences I've had in my life, and I want you to experience that. You can call me every day, and I'll be honest with you about how I'm doing. And we'll always be close, but I don't want to interrupt your life and cause you to make the wrong decisions because of my illness."

Missy listens intently, tears leaking out the sides of her serious brown eyes, hands still clutching my hands.

"They'll have to drag me kicking and screaming because I will not give up my life for cancer," I say defiantly, fishing a crumpled pink Kleenex out of my jeans pocket. "I have so much to live for—Daddy, Jordan, and you, my very precious and loving daughter."

Missy puts her arms around my neck and hugs me tight. Cornell just lost one of the top students they would ever get. What a mistake they made in wait-listing her. And yet I know this is how her story, our story, is meant to go, and I'm just grateful to be here to share her good news and know where her new home will be.

CHAPTER 9

Duck Pond

Marisa / Sally

I drive to the duck pond where my mom used to take us as kids. We'd toss them bits of white bread and then sit on a bench to eat our peanut butter sandwiches. It was a picturesque scene until one day a goose tried to bite my brother. After that we stopped going.

Tony asked me to meet him here, said we needed to talk. I'm pretty sure I know what about. All his friends have been telling me he's in love with me. They say that's why he's been coaxing me to take him to prom, telling me how much fun we'll all have. I guess secretly I've known this. I guess secretly I'm a little bit in love with him, too. More impossible-to-handle feelings, like the ones about my mom that I've been swallowing down.

Closing my car window against the chilly May day, I take the long route to the pond, stalling for time. But I find it's not Tony I'm thinking of; it's Wilson. Can I really give him up? Can I really give up on him? While stuck at a traffic light, a memory strikes me: Wilson and I showering together for the first time when I visited him last semester. Smothering giggles, we tiptoed into the men's bathroom of his dorm after midnight. He undressed shyly and stepped into the shower stall, adjusting the temperature and waiting for me to join him. I don't know what scared me more: Wilson seeing me naked, or some random dude from his dorm walking in. Panicked, I kept glancing at the door while I quickly shed my clothes in a pile on the floor, then hopped into the stall and closed the curtain behind me. I looked down at the filthy square tiles, heart pounding behind my embarrasingly bare breasts. It was the first time Wilson and I were naked together with the lights on, rendering us both shy and self-conscious. I was so nervous that I couldn't stop shivering, despite the steam of the shower. "You're beautiful," he said softly, his hand on my cheek, lifting my face so my eyes met his. "Not because of how you look naked, but because you'd show yourself to me." Clinging to each other in the small shower stall, short strands of his recently dyed blue-green hair shedding onto his bony shoulders and chest, I felt safe and loved. My parents and friends think Wilson— painfully quiet, socially awkward—isn't right for me. But they don't know these moments where he's so sincere and honest and loving. And with the long distance, and how absent he's been from The Stuff With My Mom, sometimes I forget he's that way, too. But when I remember, it makes it so much harder to know what to do.

When I pull up to the pond, Tony's black boat of a vehicle— some kind of Cadillac that resembles a hearse—is already parked. Like Tony, it's loud and ridiculous and impossible to miss. *Here I am, with all my flaws*, it seems to say. I guess that's what I love about being with Tony: the ability to be all the different sides of me. The punk rock drummer who can hang with the boys. The girly-girl *Dawson's Creek* fanatic. The chick he likes regardless of her look, whether it's contacts and gelled curls down her back, or wire-rimmed glasses and a frizzy bun. And, maybe one day, the girl whose mom is sick, the girl whose world is shattered, the girl who has never been more terrified in her life.

Sometimes I wonder if Tony knows. He did come with me once to see my mom in the hospital, a quick stop-in on our way to watch my cousin Susi's soccer game. But I was kind of vague about why she was there ("chemo" and "cancer" were still too scary to say out loud). Mostly, I was relieved to have someone there to crack a joke or two, and lighten the mood. He even brought her a single red rose.

Every so often Tony asks how my mom is, and I shrug and say she's OK, then quickly change the subject. I'm still not ready to tell him, even though lately I've considered it, the words nearly falling from my mouth until I suck them back in. The thought of sharing with Tony what's really going on is both freeing and frightening. I know the wall I keep up with Wilson will come tumbling down with Tony.

Getting out of the car, I realize I know what I want to do, and I know what I need to do. Problem is, they're two different things.

Tony's sitting on a bench staring out into the pond, and I slide in next to him, the sleeve of his soft black T-shirt brushing my shoulder.

"Oh, hey," he says, jumping slightly.

"Hi," I say, leaning over to give him a hug. It lasts a beat too long.

"God, this is so stupid," he says, breaking away.

"What do you mean?" I search his face.

"Nothing."

He's silent. I squint at the pond, looking for baby ducks. But dusk is settling, making it hard to see anything at all. I bite a nail nervously.

"I mean, do you even like me?" he blurts out finally. He seems pissed.

"I..."

"Forget it."

"You didn't even give me a chance—"

"No, really, it's fine."

"Tony..."

"I'm sorry. I'm being an asshole."

"No, you're not. Well, you kind of are, but, it's just…"

"Look, Marisa, I'm not good at this stuff. I just wanted to tell you that I think you're cool. Shit man, you're fucking awesome. And I think it totally sucks that you have a boyfriend."

Silence. This time, my own. I stare at the ducks, who seem to mindlessly choose their path through the water, and I wish I were as careless as them. Then I could just follow my heart, and not my mindfuck of a head.

"I'm sorry," I say finally, in a soft, weak voice that doesn't sound like mine. "I do have a boyfriend—and I'm not ready to let that go."

I feel his shoulders sag, hear his breath let out, a mix of anguish and the relief of having an answer. He paws at his eyes, and I realize he's brushing away tears.

"But for the record…I think you're fucking awesome, too," I say softly.

I lean against him, and he wraps an arm around me, and I press my face against his soft black T-shirt like I've longed to forever. It's the softest cotton I've ever felt. He is warm and familiar and loving, and my heart is racing. So is his; I can feel it through his shirt.

We stay like that for a while, in complete stillness, just us and the ducks, until it gets dark and we're shivering. And then we each drive home. I don't know what he does, but I cry the whole way.

Marisa / **Sally**

M issy comes home late and is quiet at dinner, moving her tuna croquettes around on her plate and not laughing at any of the lines on *Seinfeld*. I worry she's turned against me again, but I wonder if it's something else.

She told me that after school she was seeing Tony, the singer in her band. She's been spending an awful lot of time with him lately, on the phone, at band practice each week, at lunchtime, and often hanging out with him in a big group on the weekends.

He's a nice young man, don't get me wrong. As sweet as they come, from a nice Italian family, and so friendly each time he comes by the house. I was floored when he came with Missy to visit me at the hospital during a round of chemo and even brought me flowers. I was surprised she'd confided in him, especially since Missy was still keeping my illness a secret from almost all of her friends. But I instantly saw how much he cared for Missy, even if she couldn't quite admit it.

When the topic did come up a few weeks ago (she griped that everyone was pressuring her to take Tony to the prom), I tried to impart some wisdom. "Tony's a nice guy," I said, perched at the top of the staircase outside my bedroom. "But you need someone who's intellectually stimulating, someone who challenges you."

A terrible thing to say, I know, but born of a mother's want for everything for her daughter. Missy had just been ranked fourth in her graduating class, would soon be going off to a wonderful college. Their lives would go in two different directions.

"He *is* smart, Mom!" Missy shot back, standing at the bottom of the stairs, planted outside her bedroom door in case she decided to retreat. "He's in college and he's going to be a famous animator one day."

If I were being totally honest, it isn't just the smart thing. Missy has confided in me that he's depressed. That some days at band practice he's sullen and withdrawn, at times getting angry and telling off the other guys. I think part of Missy likes him because she's depressed, too—because of me.

I can tell Missy and Wilson have been drifting apart. The calls have dwindled (he isn't a "phone person," she says), and so has her time talking to him on the computer. She used to infuse him into every conversation and now she speaks of him less often. I know that losing him scares her. But the last thing she needs is another boyfriend who will soon be long distance. Another boy holding her back.

It's not like I want Missy to wait until she's thirty-four to meet someone, like her *alteh kocker* (that's "old fart" in Yiddish) mom. I just wished to instill in her my sense of optimism—that the world is so big and filled with wonderful people to meet.

I believed that even in my younger years. Once, single in my late twenties and out to dinner with my college roommate Bonnie and her husband Arnie, the waiter had asked if a fourth would be joining us. "Yes!" I'd answered brightly. "We just haven't selected him yet." I had faith that I'd find the right man, and I did.

Even today, I meet so many amazing people every day, just talking to strangers in the grocery line. Bill jokes that I have a "Talk to Me" sign on my forehead. But people just seem compelled to tell me their life stories while unloading their deli turkey and Tropicana orange juice. And, truth be told, I love to listen.

But tonight I can tell Missy is in no mood to tell me what's going on or to have me listen. She'll come to me when she's ready, I reassure myself. I excuse her from clearing the table, and she rushes upstairs. I don't know whether to call a friend or cry or both.

If only Missy would believe in herself, know how special she is, that she deserves the very best, both in guys and in life. But I suppose some of that wisdom comes only with age. So I just have to pray that I've taught her enough so far, or that I can continue to beat the odds and stick around longer so I can teach her more.

CHAPTER 10

Graduation

Marisa / Sally

I hate this dress, I think, scrutinizing my reflection in the full-length mirror in my bedroom. But I have to wear white. Our school colors are blue and white, so at graduation the boys wear blue robes and the girls wear white robes—which means any other dress color would show through the robe. It's so stupid. But apparently it's a thing.

"I don't want to wear white," I whined to Laura on the phone last month.

"I know," she said. "You *never* wear white."

"That's because I'm, like, so pale I'm practically albino." Laura's Italian year-round tan would look great against white, of course.

She laughed. "Marisa. You're not albino."

"Yes I am," I pouted. "Can't I just wear maroon or black? Who cares if it shows through?"

"Nooo!" she said, horrified. "That is totally tacky. Remember when we went to our brothers' graduations? The girls who did that just looked dumb."

"Fine!" I said, exasperated. Laura's rulebook was full of laws like

No White After Labor Day, Boys Shouldn't Wear Pleated Pants, and Shopping at Salvation Army Is Gross. But, on the graduation dress color rule, I did kind of agree with her.

"You'll find something you like," she reassured me. "We're graduating! Your mind is *not* going to be on your dress."

She was right—kind of. A week after our call, I came home from school to find a white dress laid out on my bed as a surprise.

"I found it at Marshall's!" Mom squealed, appearing in my bedroom doorway. "It was the only one they had *and* it was your size—on the clearance rack for only $9.99! I couldn't believe it! It was meant to be! It was just *waiting* for you. Do you like it?"

She was so excited. How could I have said no?

And the truth is, even though I really, *really* hate wearing white (I don't even want to wear white at my own wedding!), it's a pretty dress.

Looking in the mirror again, I try to focus on the things I love about the dress: thin spaghetti straps, low-cut neckline that shows just a drop of cleavage, a flowing skirt that gives it a hippie feel. With my dark hair in long waves, I feel like a flower child from the '60s.

But there's one major problem: the body that's inside the dress. Ever since my mom got sick, I...well...I got fat. I mean, I've always been super scrawny, so my version of fat isn't even really fat. But I can't sit through thirty minutes of Yearbook without stuffing my face full of junk food, my favorite gray cords are so tight I can barely button them, and I finally understand why women wear black when they want to look skinny—because white totally sucks!

I might have even bucked the white trend entirely, except for the fact that Mom hand-picked this dress especially for me, at a time when I didn't even know if she'd make it to the ceremony. And for the important events, like prom and graduation, I need my mom to choose these dresses. Even if I don't always like what she likes, her final approval is the way I know if the dress is right—if the whole event will be right. If it wasn't so morbid, I'd ask her to go wedding dress shopping with me tomorrow—even though I'm nowhere near getting married—just to know on that day that she will be with me. In the mirror, my dark eyes pool with tears. She's made it almost six months, well past the initial two-month diagnosis, but how much longer can we really have left? I know I should feel thankful that she even made it to graduation today, but instead I anxiously fast-forward and worry if she'll make it to prom in just a few days, or my eighteenth birthday in July, or the first day of college in August…

"Missy, are you almost ready?" Mom calls from the hall. "We have to leave in five minutes and Daddy wants to take pictures!"

Crap. I can't be red-eyed and mascara-streaked when I go downstairs, or Mom will start crying, too. I try to blot away my tears without ruining my makeup, hoping my eyes look shimmery-excited instead of shimmery-sad. Am I really graduating from high school today? Part of me can't wait to go to a big school where I'll be anonymous, walking among twenty thousand students who have no idea about my mom. But part of me fears I'll be lost, that my sadness will bury me beneath the snow and no one there will know how much I need to be saved.

"Miss!" Mom calls again with more urgency.

I grab my bag and rush downstairs. It's time to go.

Marisa / Sally

She comes down the stairs and my breath catches. Missy rarely ever wears white, and with her snow-white skin and pitch-black hair, she looks like an angel.

"Oh, Missy," I say. My eyes fill up. Then again, they do that a lot lately.

I wait for her to chastise me for being my weepy self, but she gives me that big Missy smile—the first I've seen directed at me in a long time. I guess on graduation day, with so much pressure to grow up, a daughter needs to be reminded she's still someone's little girl.

Feeling bold, I hold my arms open to her for a hug. She comes right over and holds me tight.

"Oh!" I blurt out, overcome. In that moment, Missy feels like mine again.

Just as quickly, she pulls away and straightens her dress.

"Where's Dad?" she says, looking around the living room, purposely avoiding my eyes. "We're going to be late."

"Outside, on the deck," I say. "Go ahead. I'll be out in a minute."

The screen door slams behind her, and I pretend to busy myself cleaning up the kitchen. Truthfully, I'm composing myself. Today is going to be a trying day. I feel so proud of Missy, and so thankful to be alive to celebrate her graduation. But what about her first day of college, the day she gets married, gives birth to her first child? None of us can live forever, but if the stats about pancreatic cancer are true—if even making it to this six-month mark is such a miracle—how will I be able to leave my family? My work here is not done.

"Sal!" I hear Bill yell my name from the deck. Picture time. I blow my nose and head outside.

"Pose with Missy," Bill instructs. I put an arm around Missy's shoulder and squeeze her toward me.

"Mom!" Missy whines.

"What?"

"My *hair*!" Missy whimpers and tugs her curls out from under my arm.

"Well, sor-ry!" I huff, not feeling very sorry at all.

"It's OK," she mumbles, realizing she's hurt my feelings.

"And 1...2..." Bill says.

Missy scoots near me and we give big smiles to the camera.

"3..." Bill says. A moment passes, while we stay frozen mid-pose. Then, finally, we hear the click of the shutter. We always tease him that he takes too long. Half of our photos feature one of us, usually Jordan, yelling at Bill to hurry up.

"Now you take one of me and Missy," Bill says.

"Set it up for me." I have no idea how to focus this crazy machine, especially with my thick glasses. My subjects are usually lucky if they make it into the frame! I look over at Bill, who's futzing with various dials. "Well, do you think it'll be ready this year?"

"No, next year!" He shoots back, muttering under his breath. Boy, everyone's edgy today—even Bill. It's no wonder. The past six months have been anything but calm. From my diagnosis to chemotherapy to Missy seeing a therapist…our family has gone from painfully normal to in pain. It hurts me to see us this way.

Bill throws a proud arm around Missy and she snuggles into his side. How simple a father-daughter relationship can be. I always admire their affectionate bond. Bill is a terrific father, only further proven by how much Missy worships him.

I take off my glasses and squint through the viewfinder. The shutter clicks.

"You didn't give us a warning," Missy complains. "I was talking!"

"Take another," Bill says.

Everyone's edgy…*and* everyone's a critic today! Hmph!

"1…" I begin. I hold my breath for a long pause, mimicking Bill, trying to make them laugh. Missy rolls her eyes.

"2…" Missy moves a hand to her hip.

"2 1/2…"

"Just take it!" Missy yells through clenched teeth and a camera-ready smile.

The shutter clicks.

"Finally! I'm going to be *so* late. Let's go."

I hand the camera to Bill, feeling equally exasperated. He smiles his warm Bill smile, telling me with his eyes that Missy is just acting out from the stress of graduation. Thank goodness I married a guidance counselor who just seems to *know* these things. As soon as I realize her attitude isn't about me (or at least not entirely about me),

I immediately feel better.

We drop Missy off in front of the school to join her classmates while Bill and I search for parking—no easy feat for latecomers like us. Finally, we find a spot and rush to the football field to take a seat in the bleachers. Jordan, who's home from college, plans to take his own car and will meet us here a little later. God forbid he sit in the bleachers and actually wait for the ceremony to start.

Calm down, Sal, I tell myself. It's so easy to let little things bother me today, but I know nothing can really get me down. After all, it's Missy's graduation, and I'm alive and here. I've already beaten the odds.

Later that night, I don't remember the valedictorian's speech. I don't remember the principal's parting words, or what color dress Missy's favorite English teacher was wearing. I just remember Missy, glowing and graceful as she walked across the stage to accept her diploma. What poise! My little Missy—a high school graduate.

CHAPTER 11

Prom

<u>Marisa</u> / Sally

Our limo is an hour late.

"What the hell's wrong with this company?" Stacey's father yells. The other twenty parents look away uncomfortably. He's been screaming for the past hour. As if that's helping.

Laura's mom was nice enough to host this pre-prom party at her house, complete with drinks, finger food, and tall green hedges that make the perfect photo backdrop. We've already taken rolls and rolls of pre-prom photos. I posed with Laura, Laura and Shari, Joanne and Natalie, and of course, Wilson, who—I should have remembered from his prom—only grows even more shy in the presence of parents, cameras, and a swarm of yapping girls.

My jaw hurts from smiling for so many photos. Mom's still wearing the big weepy grin she's had on her face all day: during my curly updo at the hair salon, in my bedroom while I put on makeup and stepped into my dress, on the car ride to Laura's. Six months have passed since that terrible January day, and other than a wig and some nausea, Mom looks sturdy and strong today, and doesn't seem to be going anywhere. I'd imagined this as a day of mourning, offering a wan smile for other parents' photos as I stared at the empty space where my mom would have been. So I keep looking at her, blinking, then looking again; I can't quite believe she's here. I feel happy one instant, terrified the next. *Today's not the day to focus on the negative,* I remind myself, as my therapist instructed me to do on big days when I'm feeling anxious. *It's prom, just let yourself have fun.*

"Finally!" Stacey's dad grumbles, throwing his hands in the air. Sure enough, a black stretch limo rounds the corner. We all wave him down furiously—as if the driver can't tell it's us by the swarm of princess dresses and tuxedos.

Kids and parents part ways. Moms shriek, "Call me to let me know you're OK!" Dads mumble, "Be safe." I scan the chaotic crowd for my own parents, and skip over to them. Dad wiggles his funny eyebrows at me. "Bye, pumpkin." Mom grabs me into a tight squeeze. "I love you so much, doll," she says quietly into my ear. "Have a terrific time." I hug her hard and close my eyes, thinking over and over again: *I'm so glad you're here.*

Prom is exactly like our seventh-grade dances, only at a ballroom in Queens that's way fancier than the school gymnasium. A DJ blasts radio hits like Britney Spears' "Hit Me Baby One More Time," and bar mitzvah classics like "The Macarena" and "The Electric Slide." Couples grind way too close together. Dramatic couples get into fights. Some dates totally ditch each other after the first dance, including poor Laura who's left high and dry by none other than our valedictorian! So much for chivalry. Wilson and I immediately welcome her into our awkward dancing duo, where she can truly showcase her booty-shaking moves.

The three of us take a break to sit at our table, drinking Shirley Temples and Cokes with some other friends from our limo, and of course that's when a slow song comes on. I wait for Wilson to ask me to dance, but instead he pulls me onto his lap, and even though I wanted that slow dance moment, there's something romantic about just being near him. The only awkward part is catching eyes across the table with Ben, one of the guys from my band, who gives me a funny look as if by being here with Wilson I'm cheating on Tony. I look out the big windows at the lit-up Queens skyline and wonder if Tony would have asked me to slow dance. The truth is, it wouldn't have mattered. I would have felt comfortable dragging him out to the floor regardless. Wilson hugs his arms around my waist, and I try to shrug off the feeling that no matter who I'm with, I'm hurting someone.

After prom, the eighteen of us pile back into the limo. We have an hour to kill before Dawn Delirium, a school-sponsored event where they raffle away a car. It's basically the school's way to make sure we're not drinking and driving or getting into other trouble. Since we're already in Queens, we'd all decided to take the hour to go to Manhattan. We cheer as our limo driver heads toward the South Street Seaport. I love the city and can't wait to be there unchaperoned.

On the way to the city, we break out the alcohol we'd each managed to smuggle past our parents and the limo driver. My girlfriends and I drink fruity wine coolers while the boys chug beer. Wilson reaches into his messenger bag and unfolds his hoodie. Out emerges a bottle I've never seen before.

"What is that?" I ask, intrigued and a little intimidated.

"Goldschlager." He holds up the bottle for me to see. "See? It has little gold specks, but you can drink them."

He takes a swig and passes it to me. I take a tiny sip and cough as it burns my throat, making him laugh. He offers it to my friends, but most pass. The tipsy couples in the limo start cuddling or kissing. I lean back and hold Wilson's hand, happy he agreed to come with me even though I know he really hates prom.

The limo slows and comes to a stop. I look outside—we're here! We all hide our bottles, clamber out of the limo, and immediately race toward the marina. Giddy with post-prom excitement and the fact that we have practically the whole marina to ourselves, small groups split up and run in different directions. Wilson grabs my hand and we climb up the non-working escalator until we reach the third floor balcony. Our friends tiny beneath us, the massive ships before us. Life seems so open.

"We never got to slow dance," I pout, half-playful, half-serious.

I turn away from Wilson and rest my arms on the balcony ledge. Lights from the South Street Seaport cast glittery pockets onto the East River, reminding me of the millions of sequins and strobe lights at prom. I turn back to Wilson.

He holds out his right arm in the traditional slow-dance stance.

"Now?!" I ask, incredulous.

He raises his eyebrows, revealing amused dark eyes.

"There's no music!" I laugh, latching onto his hand and snuggling up against him. We dance in silence for a moment.

He begins singing "I Want It That Way," a boy band pop song he only likes ironically, and I burst out laughing.

"We are not slow dancing to Backstreet Boys!" I protest.

He laughs that loud chuckle I love and continues singing, butchering the ballad with his gravelly voice and tinge of a Chinese accent.

I look around, but we're the only couple on the balcony. Down below, I hear our friends running around and laughing. No one knows we're up here. Everyone's too hyper and caught up in their own worlds.

Meanwhile, Wilson is a fearless singer, belting out the lyrics in a way that's totally out of character for his shy nature. Maybe it's the Goldschlager; maybe it's the magic of prom. But I secretly wish he were always this way.

Suddenly, my high-heeled feet stumble beneath me. Wilson decided to try an old-fashioned dip, but we were way too clumsy for such a classy move. Instead, we crack up. For a too-cool college freshman who didn't even rent a tux until yesterday, Wilson is a much better date than I'd expected. I breathe into his lapels and close my eyes.

Marisa / **Sally**

The limo drives away and I miss her already, even though she'll be home tomorrow. And this is just prom. How will I handle it when we drop her off at college, when I won't see her for months at a time? I tell myself not to jump too far ahead.

When Bill and I get home, the first thing I do is take off my wig. Beautiful as it may be, it's itchy and surprisingly heavy. I'm relieved to return it to the strange Styrofoam head in my walk-in closet.

Fortunately, my family has grown accustomed to how I look without the wig. So I switch into a comfortable, gray terry cloth turban. You don't even have to tie it, just plop it on your head. Ahh, that's better. I'd go without it, but my head gets cold. You'd be surprised by how much warmth your hair provides!

Settling in to watch some TV in bed, I say a little prayer for Missy. I hope she has a wonderful prom. I hope Wilson's a good date. I hope they're safe. It's all I can do these days: hope.

CHAPTER 12

Separation Anxiety

Marisa / Sally

I push the shopping cart through the automatic doors, leading the way, with Mom and Dad trailing slightly behind me. I'm panicked, but trying to act like I know what I'm doing. Trying to act like the grown-up college girl I'm about to become.

Luckily, I have a cheat sheet: the Bed Bath & Beyond circular that was mailed to our house last week. Not only does it contain a coupon for twenty percent off (the equivalent of winning the lottery to my discount-loving dad), it also includes a College Packing Checklist. Clutching the list now, I scan the zillions of items: extra-long twin sheet set, comforter, bed lifts, towels, bathrobe, shower caddy, dry erase board...

When I look up, the store is equally overwhelming. The silver shelves seem to reach up to heaven, with each row containing something out of reach, yet utterly necessary to college survival. I shiver in the air-conditioned space, buttoning my jean jacket despite the ninety-degree day outside. How will I do this? How will I leave my mom with everything going on? Where's the College Packing When

Your Mom Has Cancer Checklist, which includes copious boxes of Kleenex, the superpowers of X-ray vision to make sure she's OK and the ability to teleport home in case of emergency—oh, and don't forget the must-have panic button.

My thoughts are interrupted by a sharp scrape against the back of my ankles as a shopping cart bangs into me.

"Ow!" I shout, spinning around to find the culprit: Mom, looking tiny and adorable behind the massive cart.

"I thought maybe we'd need two," Mom says apologetically.

I try to turn my scowl into a small smile, to show I forgive her. At my appointment earlier this week, the therapist predicted today would be hard for both of us. And that it would be up to me to prevent a blowup.

We recover and head to our first stop: bedding. Since my dorm room will be so small, the comforter and sheets will dictate the look of everything else, Mom explains.

"Ooh, Missy, look at these!" Mom says, casually ripping opening the plastic package of leopard print sheets. "They're jersey cotton and really soft."

"Mom!" I hiss, mortified, looking up and down the aisle. "You can't just open them!"

"How else can you tell if they're soft?" she says. "Besides, no one's around. And what are they going to do? Arrest the woman with cancer?"

I have to admit she has a point. But still I look around to make sure no managers are nearby, and no customers have heard her say the C word.

Convinced we're safe, I reach my hand in and touch the fabric. They *are* really soft, and the pattern seems to fit my punk rock, drummer girl style. I try to picture Wilson visiting for a weekend and sleeping over in my dorm room, but my brain wanders to Tony. "I can, like, come visit you and stuff, right?" he'd asked shyly—but that was before the duck pond. Now everything feels different. We still have band practice and lunch together, but he won't quite meet my eyes. Mom keeps trying to not-so-subtly hint that maybe neither guy is right for me—not Wilson and not Tony either—and that I'll meet so many new people in college. But the thought of being with someone brand new, who doesn't know me and doesn't know my mom, somehow sounds lonelier than being alone. Realizing I'm still petting the sheets, I pull my hand away.

"I love them," I say now to Mom. She beams and drops a fresh, unopened package into the cart. I can tell she's thrilled that she's picked out something I like, the same way she reacted when choosing my prom and graduation dresses. I have to give her these small moments. Thank God my mom has fun taste or I'd be filling my dorm room with flowered curtains and doilies.

We choose another sheet set in maroon, and a plain black comforter after realizing every other color looks hideous with leopard print. Maybe *The Nanny* could pull that off, but I can't!

Two hours later, all of us cranky and exhausted, Dad piles the trunk with everything on the College Packing Checklist. Driving home, I realize there's no turning back now. I guess I'll have to go to college.

Marisa / Sally

As we drive home, the trunk and backseat filled with items that will soon fill Missy's dorm room, I get a premonition of driving her to college two months from now. I see us sitting in the same poses: Bill driving, me in the passenger seat, Missy in the backseat behind me. I dread the moment of dropping her off at school, of saying goodbye, but I find myself smiling: I know I'll be there.

CHAPTER 13

Midnight Chats

Marisa / Sally

It's fifteen minutes past my midnight curfew, but my parents aren't the type to wait up. Besides, they know I'm just at the diner with Laura and Natalie. So I'm sure everyone will be asleep once I get home.

That's why I jump when I see Mom sitting at the kitchen table.

"Mom!" I gasp. "You scared me."

"Hi, Miss," she says, smiling weakly. Her favorite mug—the outside decorated with tiny red hearts, an "I love you" at the bottom visible only once you finish your tea—is filled with her usual Lemon Soother. A box of saltines sits on the table in front of her. The TV isn't on. She's just been sitting, staring, thinking.

"You're still up…" I say.

"I couldn't sleep," Mom says. "My back was hurting…I just couldn't get comfortable."

"Oh," I say, thinking it's funny that we still feel more comfortable blaming the back pain, her first symptom. Not cancer, not chemo, not anxiety. Just a minor backache, like in an Advil commercial.

"So!" she says, perking up. "Did you have fun?"

"Yeah," I say, plopping down on the kitchen chair next to hers. "Well, kind of. Everyone's stressed about boys."

"Oh?"

"Well, Laura hung out with this guy, but he usually only hangs out with popular girls, so she doesn't know if he's going to ask her out again or not."

"That's crazy! Of course he will. Laura's a great catch."

"I'm not saying she isn't," I groan. "But it doesn't always work that way. I know it was like a hundred years ago, but don't you remember high school?"

Mom laughs and swats me with her paper napkin. "It was *not* a hundred years ago, thankyouverymuch. But I know high school can be very cliquey. It won't be like that in college."

"Thank God!" I say. Even though I'm scared to leave my family and friends, and continue to be far away from Wilson, part of me can't wait to go to college, where even if a few close friends know about my mom, it doesn't mean the whole school has to know.

"You're gonna love it, you know," she says.

"I hope so," I mumble.

"Please!" she says. "Just think—you already know your college roommate! You already have one friend! And she seems like a real sweetheart."

I think about Linda. It seemed fated that we'd be roommates. My mom's close friend Nikki, who lives a few towns over, first suggested it, telling my mom that the girl next door was also going to Syracuse. Then my friend Dan told me his best friend from childhood was going to Syracuse and wanted to find a roommate. Mom and I couldn't believe both of them were talking about the same person— Linda. So, Dan and Linda and I went one night to The Beanery, my favorite coffee place, to meet and decide if we wanted to room together. We joked that it felt like a blind date! She wants to be an art teacher and loves singing and acting. I want to be a writer and love playing drums. The artist and the writer, both musicians. At the end of the night, we both said yes, giggling and hugging and talking about who would bring the microwave.

"What if we end up hating each other?" I ask my mom now. She warned me to stay away from catty girls throughout my childhood, but I was often sucked in by their popularity and confidence. Finally, in middle and high school, I learned from my mistakes and gained a group of friends who were the nicest girls in the world. Linda seems nice, too…but what if she's not? And I'll have to see her *every single day*.

"Oh, Missy, you just have to hope for the best," Mom says with an exasperated sigh. "Since when are you such a pessimist?"

She's right. I've always been an optimist. Dad says that as a little girl I woke up giggling, and Mom says my smile "lights up a room." When did that change? I know it has something to do with Mom being sick, but I fear this new me is taking over, sneaking over my skin one inch at a time. I don't want to lose who I've been for the past seventeen years. Without that, who am I anyway?

"I know," I say. "I'm sure it'll be fine. She did seem really nice."

I grab a few saltines and stack them like blocks, trying to imagine this whole new world I'm about to enter.

"What's going on with Wilson?" Mom asks. "I haven't seen him in a while."

"He's fine," I stall, taking a bite. She's trying to make the question sound casual, but I can tell she's fishing for information. How does she always know when things with him are off?

"Fine?" Mom asks. Did I really think she'd drop it so easily?

"I dunno," I mumble. "We kind of got into a fight."

"Really?" Mom says, surprised. "When? What happened?"

"When we went to Warped Tour last weekend," I say.

"Of course! Standing outside in the heat all day, caked in mud! Any couple would want to kill each other," Mom jokes. She doesn't really understand my music scene, how much I love the loud songs drowning out my thoughts—but she always knows how to make me laugh. "I'm only kidding, Miss, you know that. What happened?"

"He was just bothering me. I was tired so I sat down on the ground to take a break, and he kept poking me on the top of my head. And finally I couldn't take it anymore and yelled at him."

"You *yelled*? What did you say?"

I cringe and look down at the table. "I said, 'You're so annoying!'"

"Oh, Missy! You didn't!"

"I know, it's so mean," I say, feeling my cheeks turn red.

"What did he say?"

"He was really pissed. He said 'Fine!' and just kind of walked off."

"He left you by *yourself*?"

"No, I wasn't by myself—there were like a million people there," I say. She's so overdramatic. "I just kind of walked around, and listened to some bands, and hung out with Natalie and Tony and that group."

"Oh, Tony was there," Mom says slowly, starting to understand.

"Yeah," I say flatly. I can't meet her eyes.

"Is that why you got into a fight with Wilson?"

"I dunno. Probably."

"Missy…"

"I know it's not nice," I say. "But I just kept wishing all day that I was there with them instead. And Wilson's so quiet that it's weird to all hang out as a group."

"It's hard," Mom agrees. "He's such an introvert, and you're so social."

"I know! But then I felt really bad and went looking for Wilson. And he was just walking around looking totally miserable."

"Poor Wilson," Mom clucks her tongue.

"I apologized. I said, 'I'm sorry for calling you annoying.' He said he was upset because kids used to tell him he was annoying when he was little."

"Did he forgive you?"

"I don't know. Sort of? It was just still kind of awkward after that. And it hasn't really been the same since."

"Well, sometimes a break gives you time to think," Mom says. I stiffen. She's never understood him, and that sounds like her subtle way of saying we should break up.

"I guess," I mumble, molding the cracker crumbs into a tiny mountain.

"You're about to start a whole new chapter of your life, meet so many new people," Mom says—her other subtle way of saying we should break up. "Maybe you want some freedom to explore…"

"Maybe," I say, noncommittal.

Mom yawns. Her mug is empty, and it's nearly one in the morning. Ominous shadows lurk around the dining room, but I remember when sunshine used to stream in through the big bay window. When the conversation wasn't about college or boyfriends or backaches or illness, but whatever topic the kindergarten version of me babbled about back then. When Mom and I would sit at the kitchen table and share a grapefruit, sliced in half, that my mom had sectioned patiently with a knife—the one that was serrated on both sides like a shark's jaw. When the hardest decision was choosing which half of the grapefruit would be mine and which half would be hers, even though inevitably she'd shovel the pulp out of both and hold the spoon to my lips, juice dribbling down my chin as I demanded more with a giggling squeal.

"Bedtime?" Mom asks, and instead of a ripe grapefruit it's an empty mug, and instead of Mom's toothy smile it's the worry lines that frame her thin lips.

"Yeah, I guess," I say, yawning, too. It's exhausting right now to remember the past, to recall with shock how everything has changed.

I get up and hug her without her asking, resting my head on her bony shoulder. I wonder if she still thinks I'm a bad kid—if I *am* a bad kid—for running away and ignoring her for all those months. "I love you, Mom," I whisper.

"I love you, too, my precious doll," she says. "I love you so much."

Marisa / **Sally**

I lie in bed, but can't sleep. She said "I love you," right? I didn't imagine it?

As a little girl, Missy was the most affectionate daughter you could ask for. She loved hugs so much that when she reached out to her kindergarten teacher on a particularly warm day, the poor woman exclaimed, "Isn't it too hot for a hug?" But I had no such limits and welcomed Missy hugs in the morning when she woke up, in midafternoon just because, while I was cooking dinner, and before she went to sleep.

Naturally, her hug quota lessened as she became a teenager, when sometimes my outstretched arms were met with, "Ma, enough!" But still, on her time, and especially if she was upset, she would crawl into my bed and rest her head on my chest.

Since I've become sick, it sometimes feels like she's afraid to come too close. Maybe she thinks I'm too fragile and will break. Maybe she thinks cancer is contagious. Maybe she just wants to avoid it all—that last one's my hunch.

So to get a hug and an "I love you" tonight, unprovoked, made my day. She's coming back to me. I can feel it.

CHAPTER 14

Reflections

<u>Marisa</u> / Sally

I t's a place we love. A place we go, just the two of us. A holy place.
It's the Gap.

So when Mom knocks softly on my bedroom door this afternoon
and asks if I want to go, I cut off Laura mid-story and hang up the
phone. Grabbing my wallet and stuffing in some money I'd saved
from my gig as a mother's helper this summer, I step into my maroon
flip-flops and rush downstairs.

Mom's waiting by the front door, car keys in hand. "Ready?" she
asks, flashing me a sparkling smile. It feels so much like old times
that the déjà vu nearly knocks me over. Before Mom got sick, she'd
often come home from work and call up the stairs, "Miss, ya wanna
go to the Gap?" Knowing I'd say yes, she'd never even pause to take
off her coat. But we haven't gone much since…everything.

I feel lost in time as Mom drives down the main road in our
town. Shopping is a well-loved mother-daughter tradition, especially
on Long Island, but our trips to the Gap are about so much more.
Running local errands are among the rare times it's just Mom and

me. Ever since the Great Speeding Ticket of 1969, Mom's been petri-fied of highway driving, so longer trips to the mall or New York City require Dad to chaperone. Even though I love my time with both parents, nothing's more fun than hanging out alone with Mom, who's even more hilarious when it's just the two of us. Dressing rooms inevitably become comedy shows, with Mom as the star and me as her giggling audience.

Comedy's harder to come by these days. Ever since Mom got sick, her desire to go to the Gap has waned. She doesn't need work clothes, she doesn't like the way she looks, and she doesn't want to run into acquaintances who will ask nosy questions or gossip about her later. But today's different. It's a few weeks before I leave for Syra-cuse, and even though it's August, Mom wants to get me some warm clothes for winter.

After a short car ride, quiet but content, Mom and I arrive at our Mecca. We flip through the racks, drawn to the same items, pulling size XS for me and S for her. We've never minded dressing alike. One Gap trip found us in matching black wintry vests, mine trimmed with brown lamb's wool, hers with gray. Another time the mirror reflected us in jean overalls with matching thermal striped shirts underneath. For many years, Mom even had a perm to match my natural curls. If a saleslady commented that we looked like sisters, it just made us giggle more.

Today the dressing room again finds us modeling matching garb—sporty navy capris and plain white tees—but we're no longer mistaken for twins. Mom looks more like my little tomboy sister, with her tiny face sheltered by a blue baseball cap to hide her thinning hair, the long remaining strands a whisper down her back, making her look like a rock star has-been. But she can't bear to part with those locks, and I understand they're her only normal left. When she asked if she should shave them off a few weeks ago, I said, "No, Mom, it looks fine." It's my only normal, too.

Mom studies me as I pull on a heavy gray hoodie intended for

Syracuse's snowy winters. For the first time, it's an item she doesn't need, and I'm an entity apart from her. The umbilical cord cut by cancer, by college, by the unstoppable force of growing up.

She's always longed to keep me her little girl. The night before every birthday, Mom would tuck me in and scold me playfully, "I thought I told you not to get any older, Missy." "Mom!" I'd squeal, "I *have to* get older." But before falling asleep I'd worry about turning nine or ten or eleven, because it seemed to make Mom so sad.

Today it's the hoodie that breaks her heart. "Missy, what am I going to do without you?" she asks. I look down, not wanting to catch her eye, not even in the mirror, not trusting myself not to fall apart in the Gap dressing room, of all places. A friend's chatty mom works here and I do *not* need her witnessing a meltdown.

Mom puts an arm around my waist and I drape one across her tiny shoulders, the few long strands of her hair tickling my hand. A wave of remorse rushes through me as I tower over her, bursting with health and youth.

The night before I turned twelve, I told Mom that she couldn't tell me not to get older anymore. "It makes me feel so guilty," I said. "Oh Missy, I was only teasing…sort of," she said. "You'll understand one day when you have children. Part of you will never want them to grow up. But I *do* want you to grow up, Missy. I want to see all the wonderful things you become, my precious doll."

I feel the same guilt now. I know part of Mom doesn't want me to grow up, doesn't want me to go to college, wants me forever with her. Part of me wants that, too. But the other part of me wants to run away from home, get away from my parents and illness and small-town gossip, leave behind Laura and Wilson and Tony, and explore this side of me that's aching to get out.

At my final therapy session with Rosie last week I confessed, "I just…I *want* to like it, I *want* to be happy there. I'm just scared. What if I'm not? Or what if something happens to her and I'm not here?" And I cried, just as Rosie had predicted I would from the beginning, rolling my eyes as she leaned over to hand me that stupid box of Kleenex. But it felt good, too. Like some sort of breakthrough.

A few weeks later my room is filled with duffle bags and Hefty garbage bags and cardboard boxes, the pink carpet barely visible. I know there's no turning back. I have to grow up. I have to go.

Marisa / <u>Sally</u>

Missy's out with Wilson tonight, saying goodbye before Bill and I drive her up to school tomorrow, and walking past her bedroom breaks my heart. All those bags, her favorite photos taken off the walls and packed away, a room about to be stripped bare.

"Don't you want to hold onto her and keep her close?" Bonnie had asked me after Missy accepted the offer to go to Syracuse. College roommates at the University of Connecticut years ago, Bonnie and I had both been far from home for the first time and knew the importance of that experience. Still, she was shocked by my firmness, so soon after my diagnosis, that Missy go away to college as planned. But my pride had surpassed my selfishness. Missy had worked so hard her entire school career, and she deserved to attend that elite program in journalism.

For my generation, women's career options were so limited: secretary, nurse, teacher. I'd chosen special education just to differentiate myself in some way. I loved my career, but sometimes I imagined an alternate life as a genetic counselor, helping older moms like me navigate frightening results from pregnancy testing. Math and science were never my strong suits, so who knows if I could have handled the schooling required. But it was more the idea of an untraditional role that excited me. Why should only men have that opportunity?

From the time Missy was little, I'd told her she could do anything, be anything. When the endless options seemed to overwhelm her, we took out books from the library about all the jobs that exist. How could I hold her back now, at the pivotal moment when she leaves the nest?

Bonnie understands, of course. She also has two children, lovely girls who are both away in college. When I called her months ago to tell her my diagnosis, she gasped.

"Don't worry, I'm going to beat it!" I told her, bursting with optimism.

Bonnie couldn't believe I was comforting her. But at the time I felt so confident that in the battle of pancreatic cancer versus Sally, I would most certainly win. Now, eight months later, I'm not so sure. Tonight, more than anything, I feel overcome with sadness that I may not witness much of Missy's college experience or her college graduation. I will see her off, and I am thankful for that, but it feels like a book I might not finish reading.

When Missy first applied to schools, before my diagnosis, my biggest concern was empty nest syndrome. For the first time since that one summer the kids went to sleepaway camp, both Jordan and Missy would be out of the house, and Bill and I would be on our own. That worry seems ridiculous now. How will Bill and I have time to sit around and cry that both kids aren't around anymore when he's still working full-time and I have chemo every two to three weeks, recovery days and nasty side effects, frequent doctor's visits, routine blood tests and MRIs and CAT scans. The list goes on and on. I want to tell everyone I've found the cure for empty nest syndrome: cancer!

I linger in Missy's bedroom doorway, taking in the dirty pink carpet, the unmade bed with the crumpled floral spread, the clothing strewn on the floor. The mess I've nagged her about for eighteen years. Starting tomorrow, her room will be spotless, and yet my heart will be broken. Will Missy feel the same way one day, gazing at my empty chair, or my empty side of the bed, or the empty space I've left in her heart?

I told Missy to go. I told her not to let me stop her. I know I was right.

And yet I miss her already.

CHAPTER 15

Syracuse

Marisa / Sally

I turn the silver-star key chain, spin it like a pistol in a cowboy Western, feeling each point of the star dig into my palm the entire drive to college. I'm too distracted to read, and I don't want to talk to my parents. I don't want to tell them what I did last night.

Two hours into the five-hour drive, we stop to eat at a diner. Unwilling to part with the key chain, I put it in the back pocket of my jeans. The corners jut into my butt, but I refuse to move it. I don't want my parents to ask about it. And I keep telling myself that I deserve it. I deserve to feel pain.

Over my Caesar salad and Dad's chicken salad sandwich and Mom's meager side salad with Russian dressing on the side, my parents talk about little nothings. The traffic, various routes, that Jordan made it up to Rhode Island last night despite leaving so late. I go to the bathroom and stare at my sad eyes in the mirror.

When I slide back into the booth, the conversation lulls and Mom studies me. *I can't believe my baby's going off to college*, her weepy expression reads.

I look away, embarrassed. Always the perfect, Goody Two-shoes, straight-A student, I don't want to confess that I don't know what the hell I'm doing. That I'm fucking everything up.

"It sounded like you were up late last night," Mom says intuitively. "How was saying goodbye to Wilson?"

"I broke up with him," I respond. My stoic voice hides my heartache.

"You did?" Mom gasps. "*Last night*?"

Dad raises his eyebrows, equally surprised.

I nod.

"And you waited all this time to tell us? Missy!"

"I...didn't know I was going to. It just kind of happened."

"Oh, Miss..." Mom begins.

Glad I transferred the star to my hoodie pocket in the bathroom, I twist the silver chain like rosary beads. If Mom's illness has taught me anything, it's to pray to anyone, all the time, with anything. *Please let me be OK, please let me be OK...*

"How did he take it?" Mom asks. "He's so sensitive."

Her comment surprises me. He's so quiet that I'm shocked she knows anything else about him. But she's right: something I've learned in the past year is that he *is* sensitive. It shows in his blog, in the mix tapes he makes for me, in the song lyrics he writes about me, in the star keychain he gave to me last night as a going-away present—which only makes me feel even worse for breaking up with him.

"He was upset," I tell Mom. *And pissed*, I add in my head. He accused me of not even giving it a try. After all, *he'd* been long distance with me *his* freshman year of college. I said we had been trying, the past year and all summer—wasn't he tired of trying? I felt so tired.

All last night, while Wilson and I were sitting on my bedroom floor surrounded by all my packed-up stuff, I kept hearing a cruel chant: *end it, end it, everything ends*. The twister that carried Dorothy away in *The Wizard of Oz* seemed to be spiraling me away, too—

from my sick mom, from my safe home, from Laura (the one friend I actually confided in). So why not from Wilson? What more could break me?

"I know you really liked him..." Mom begins.

Loved him, I correct her in my head.

"...and I know you don't want to hear this..." she continues.

Probably not.

"...but this way you'll get to meet new people," she says brightly. It sounds unsympathetic, but when I look up, her eyes only show warmth and worry. I realize it's not about whether she likes or doesn't like Wilson; she just wants the very best for me.

"I guess," I say. The thought of meeting new guys seems exhausting. How will I tell them about my mom? How will I let them in? I haven't even told Laura yet that I broke up with Wilson. I'm about to be a communications major and I'm probably the worst communicator ever.

"Let's go," Dad says, fidgeting in the booth. Mom scowls at him. She always complains that he never says goodbye before hanging up the phone...he just hangs up. He's sweet in every other aspect of life, but abrupt with goodbyes. And last night into today—and, in fact, the whole summer and maybe ever since Mom was diagnosed—is turning into one long goodbye. Will this be the last time I see her? What if something happens while I'm away? Sensing my anxiety, Dad pulls me in for a hug on our way to the car.

As we drive the rest of the way, I remind myself that Mom *wants* me to go away to school and continue on with my original plans. She'd be filled with guilt and regret if I did anything else. I have to go. I have to say goodbye.

The goodbye is less cinematic than I pictured. Linda and her parents and me and my parents are stuffed into our tiny dorm room surrounded by our suitcases, garbage bags, and boxes (Long Island girls do *not* travel light). Our parents try to help us unpack, but neither Linda nor I can handle the combination of heat, claustrophobia, and the built-up pressure from the day. Finally we shoo them away, reassuring them, "We can take it from here!" Reluctantly, the parents give in.

"Bye, pumpkin!" Dad says, giving me a big squeeze.

Mom holds me longer, whispering in my ear, "I love you, precious doll. Call me anytime, OK?"

I hug her back and force a cheerful, "I love you, too."

I push aside the thought of it being our final goodbye. I pretend it's the same as Linda saying goodbye to her mom. I do it for my sake and for Mom's, and so I don't break down.

Later that day—after Linda and I unpack (giggling over a prank note snuck in from Wilson: "Don't forget to wear clean underwear!"), after she admires my CD collection and I flip through her DVDs, after we poke our heads into other rooms and introduce ourselves to cute boys and friendly girls, after we return to our dorm room and stand in front of her computer watching funny *Saturday Night Live* skits and cracking up—I confide in her.

"Um, so, I guess you should probably know..." I say, looking down at my horribly bitten nails. "My mom is sick."

"Oh no!" she says, pausing the video and fixing her sympathetic brown eyes on me.

She only met Mom earlier that day, but instantly loved her, laughing hysterically at her fixation on Matt, our dorm's R.A., who had come by to introduce himself.

"Oh Missy, he's cute!" Mom had exclaimed. "If I were in college..."

Right at that moment Matt had walked past our open door, clearly overhearing us.

"Mom!" I'd hissed, mortified, but she and Linda were in hysterics and soon I was, too.

"What's wrong with her?" Linda asks now.

"Um, she has cancer...in her pancreas. And it's spread to her liver. So, um, it's Stage 4? Which I guess means it's pretty bad." A nervous giggle escapes, and I figure I might as well tell her everything. "Also? I broke up with Wilson last night." I'd told her about Wilson when we first met at the coffee shop.

"OK, come here," she says, matter-of-factly. "I'm going to give you a hug because that's what I do."

She opens her arms and I fall into them, relieved to have it all out in the open. We stand like this for a moment, and my brain rushes to future moments like this: bad blood test results or, worse, Mom dying. Will I be standing here with Linda hugging me? Will I always regret not being home with Mom? I try to look on the bright side: *at least someone will be there to hug me.*

Marisa / **Sally**

Once we do everything parents can possibly do on move-in day—flag down a "Goon Squad" volunteer to transport Missy's bags and boxes from our car to her room, watch from the dorm room doorway as she and Linda greet each other with a big hug and giggles of excitement, thoroughly embarrass Missy in front of her R.A. (oops!), and finally get ushered out by a suddenly grown-up Missy who insists she can unpack herself—we drive the five hours home. I congratulate myself for not crying until we leave her dorm.

In the car, I can't get over how close Missy and Linda seem to be, despite not knowing each other for very long. I think of Shirley, my first roommate at the hospital, who lost her battle with pancreatic cancer only months after we met, and yet her upbeat nature continues to inspire me. I think of my college roommate, Bonnie, who's still one of my dearest friends. I hope Missy and Linda might find that kind of connection.

But, even more so, I can't help but think about my recent room-mates. Each time I stay overnight at the hospital for chemo, I'm paired with someone new. And it's at the hospital that I've met some of the bravest people whom I've had the privilege to know. A circle of unlikely companions linked by cancer.

Sharon, my roommate earlier this month, both of us there for our usual chemo routines, was a thirty-four-year-old black woman who had suffered all the abuses a life of poverty could hand her. And yet, she had such a determined way that I hoped would help her heal and get better.

"Sally, you can't feel sorry for yourself," she told me, sitting up in her hospital bed. "You have to be brave and keep your chin up. It's your attitude that will make you or break you." I've learned this is the credo of all cancer patients who have the will to survive.

Sharon was HIV positive and also had cancer of the vagina. She told me the sad story of her life, and all I could feel was, "How much could one person endure?" She had such a bright, cheery outlook and a bubbly personality. And yet she'd been only fourteen years old when she had her son, now twenty, and later gave birth to a daughter who was now a teenager herself. She was also a grandmother to her son's child, whom she called her "baby." Sharon had been raped as a teenager, and physically and sexually abused by her stepfather when she was only a girl. So she'd turned to drugs. Her escape came in the form of crack. In becoming a drug addict, she also was introduced to the world of prostitution. When I met her, she'd given up drugs in the hope of beating her cancer so that she could at least live to see her next birthday in April. I pray she'll make it. I can't believe it's already August.

The roommate connection can be a tight, instantaneous bond. But how will Linda react to the news of my situation, and will she be able to relate to Missy? The daughter we dropped off at college is a different girl than she was eight months ago—before I was diagnosed, I think as I gaze out the car window. Though still giggling, she has a side that's serious and filled with anxiety.

Cancer robs children of their childhood. I knew all too well from my own mother's breast cancer diagnosis. And now I know from my kids' reactions to my own illness. It's a loss of innocence you can never recapture. Well—maybe when you fall in love you regain it for a while. At least I did. And I hope one day my children will experience it, too, and that I'll be around to share it with them and to marvel at their happiness. For now, Missy just has to get through her first night at college. I pray she'll be happy.

CHAPTER 16

Midnight Calls

Marisa / Sally

A few weeks after I've been away at college, our dorm room phone rings on Sunday at midnight. "It's your mom," Linda predicts, and we both crack up. Other girls on our floor get booty calls at this hour. Me? I get calls from my mother.

I roll my eyes at Linda, but secretly I love the calls. Our late night chats had continued over the summer and become almost nightly by the time I left for college, with Mom purposefully staying up late to greet me when I walked in the door. Neither of us are ready to let them go. Now that I'm at school, Mom knows if she calls late, I'm usually able to talk, having (mostly) finished my homework, but still a few hours away from sleep. College has only encouraged my night owl tendencies, since everyone else is awake, too.

"Hi, Mom!" I say upon picking up. She laughs because I know it's her without asking. I bring the phone into the hall for some privacy.

"Hi, Miss! How are you?"

"Good! How are you?" I pace the hall, excited to hear from her, unable to sit still.

"Feeling pretty good, doll."

I bask in the warmth of her voice, and the way she calls me "doll" just like her mom called her.

"How was chemo?" I ask.

"Good. I feel strong, just a little nauseous, but happy to be back home. But I have to tell you, I met the nicest young man, a nurse named Cliff, who told me about his dad who had cancer when Cliff was just a little boy. Every day he feared for his father's life—but his father lived for fifteen years!"

"Wow," I say with envy. I want those fifteen years.

"I know. He told me, 'Sally, don't live your disease. Live your life while you're waiting to get well. Because one day, you'll say, 'For the past fifteen years I've been waiting to die' instead of saying 'For the past fifteen years I've been living in the hope of surviving cancer.'"

"That's amazing, Mom." Tears blur the beige cinder block walls of the hall. I lean against the ones behind me. The sandpaper seams scrape against my back and remind me that something here is solid.

"I have to remember those words," Mom says.

"You and me both," I say, thinking of the way I'd abandoned her when we thought she had only two months to live. Being away at college—getting some physical distance from home and Mom, having phone calls where she actually feels like my closest friend—makes me feel even worse about how I reacted in the beginning.

"We will, doll," she says. "Anyway, enough of that sad talk. How's college life?"

"It's good," I say cheerfully. "I met some guys in my dorm who want to form a band together. And tonight Linda and I went to see this band Guster play at the student center for $3!"

"Oh, that sounds like fun. Have you spoken to Laura?"

"A little. We're both so busy it's hard to find time to talk."

"I'm sure. But try to make time for her, she's a good friend."

I roll my eyes even though I know she's right. "OK, Mom, I will."

"What about Wilson? Do you hear from him?"

"Yeah. We talk a lot, actually." I pause, considering how much I want to reveal. "It doesn't really feel like we're broken up."

What I don't want to admit: we've been e-mailing or talking online several times a day. And that my heart still pounds when the phone rings and his low, gravelly voice is on the other end.

"Do you want to get back together with him?" Mom asks. She sounds genuinely curious and not judgmental, like she has in the past, and I wonder if the distance between us has helped her see me more as a friend, too.

"I don't know. He wants me to come visit him next month. He says I can find cheap flights to Pittsburgh."

"That's far, Missy." I hear talking in the background. "Daddy says you'll be on one of those little propeller jets. They're very bumpy, not like a real plane. It's a little scary."

"Well, I can't take a bus or train there," I say impatiently, annoyed that she's switched back to Mom mode. "It takes like twenty hours!"

"I know, doll," she says calmly. "Let us know what you decide to do. If you feel you need to see him, I understand. He's been a part of your life for a long time."

"Yeah," I say, surprised by her level of understanding. I think back to the first time she met Wilson. He came to our house to pick me up, but I had just gotten out of the shower and wasn't ready yet. Mom entertained him, chatting with him at the kitchen table, but all she got were Wilson's shy one-word answers and mumbles. Normally able to talk to anyone, Mom was so taken aback that she kept offering him her box of Famous Amos cookies. And equally uncomfortable, Wilson kept accepting them to be nice. When we finally got into his car, I asked how it went, eager to hear what he thought of my mom. He laughed: "I really like her, but I'm so full!"

"What about at school?" Mom asks now. "Have you met anyone there?"

"Um, not really," I lie.

Kyle, from upstate New York, tried to kiss me on my second night at Syracuse. Eager to leave the stupid Ice Cream Social with all its forced friendliness, I invited him back to my dorm room, not realizing that was code to make out. We sat on my bed talking, but when he leaned in for a kiss, I jerked back, nearly hitting my head on the cinder block wall behind me. Two weeks later, Wilson told me he was seeing a show with some girl, and, in a jealous rage, I invited Kyle over again. This time when he leaned in, I kissed him back until Linda knocked on the door (per our plan), claiming she had to go to sleep. When the door closed behind him we burst into giggles, but being with someone new made me feel like crying. Taking a deep breath, I went online and confessed everything to Wilson. He was shocked and hurt. *The girl at the show was just a friend*, he typed, *and anyway she's not you*. I typed back: *This guy wasn't you either*.

"No one from your classes?" Mom presses.

How does she always know? Immediately I think of Chris, the guy in my Spanish class who I noticed on day one. Tall and handsome, outgoing and funny ("Call me Paco," he told the class), he's my first unattainable crush. The guys I like are typically nerdy and unusual, guys I know I can get. Chris is in another league. And yet there's something in his dark eyes that seems so soft and sad, reflecting my own misery over my mom. Often I accidentally gaze at him from across the classroom, my eyes filling with tears as I panic: *is my mom dying while I sit in this stupid class learning about past participle verbs?* Last week he caught me, waving a hand over his face to snap me out of it. Blushing, I looked down at my notebook, mortified. But when I glanced back up at him, something in his smile wasn't just teasing, but kind and sympathetic. I felt like he could be someone who understood an inordinate amount of sadness.

"I don't know, Mom," I say. "It's hard to start all over again when Wilson and I know each other so well." *And he knows you*, I add in my head. What if I meet someone here and they never get to meet

Mom? It seems impossible, like I'll never be able to fully let someone in, that they'll never truly know me without knowing her.

"I understand," she sympathizes.

I can tell she wants to chat longer, but from the hallway, I hear Linda turn on the TV for our nightly routine.

"Mom, do you mind if I go? Linda and I are gonna go watch Conan O'Brien before we go to sleep. Ya know, classes tomorrow, and all."

"Go, go!" Mom says, but her enthusiasm feels forced. "It's so nice to hear your voice. I'm glad you're happy there, Missy."

"Me, too," I say, letting my relief come through the phone. I know it means a lot to Mom to feel like we made the right decision—choosing Syracuse, continuing with our plan of me going away. "Seriously, I love it here."

"I'm so glad, doll. I love you."

"Love you, too, Mom."

Marisa / Sally

I hang up slowly and my smile sinks, my anxiety returns. I'm not usually a jealous person, but I envy Missy preparing for her classes tomorrow. I wish I could wake up and go to work. Wow! I never felt like that on a Sunday night—always dreaded Monday morning. Now, all I want is to be ordinary. I miss teaching and the kids and my friends and my school and even my little room in the basement. These past things defined me.

Now cancer defines me. It limits me and makes me a smaller person. The spontaneous, happy, laughing Sally is hidden behind depression. Trying to be brave, to be whole, but I'm not. Everyone around me is defined by my cancer—limited, fearful, no bursts of laughter.

Where am I? What have I done to my family? To my friends? When will I be Sally again—healthy, happy, ordinary. Wow, ordinary seems like a miracle now.

I'll always long for my health. It's how I saw myself: centered, content, happy, angry, sad. All these things, not just depressed. Not Sally who has cancer. Just regular old Sally.

Where am I? Where have I gone? Will I ever come back? And if I do, I'll never be the same. I've seen the dark side of life.

CHAPTER 17

Losing It

Marisa / Sally

In October I take that tiny bumpy jet to Pittsburgh, relieved to see Wilson waiting for me in the airport. I walk shyly over to him, and he picks me up off the ground and wraps me in a big bear hug, letting me down slowly so I feel every inch of his body. He's dyed his shaggy black hair a dark navy blue and started playing guitar in a band; I feel like I'm dating a rock star. Everyone on campus seems to know him, waving and saying hi when they see him. "These guys are even nerdier than me!" he brags, laughing. My quiet guy has transformed into a superstar.

I've changed a bit, too. Finally I'm a college student like him, and as we catch up and trade stories, I feel confident and sophisticated. For the first time, I'm his equal. During the day we walk around campus holding hands. At night we sleep intertwined in his tiny twin bed, hooking up while his roommate snores in the bed across from us.

But there's one thing we haven't done together, and even though we're not fully boyfriend and girlfriend again, we agree we want to be each other's firsts. We're not quite ready yet, but maybe over winter break, he says.

When winter break rolls around, I return home to find my mom looking different—smaller and frail and nearly bald, now with multiple wigs to choose from. To be fair, I look different, too, with my long curls chopped to just above my shoulders and an eyebrow ring poking out from above my green plastic-framed glasses. We're equally shocked by each other's looks, although Mom admits even though she usually hates piercings, she thinks I look "cute."

Meanwhile, Wilson and I hatch a plan. I'll come over to his house around 10 p.m., once his parents have gone upstairs to bed. We've never spent much time at his house, and when I park on his block I wonder if it's odd this is so planned out. In movies, the characters always seem to move flawlessly between making out and having sex. Shouldn't this be more natural or spontaneous? But I don't want to go back home, back to my death house, and I want to know what's on the other side of virginity. Cancer has forced me into adulthood. All I want is a career and a love life to go with it. Maybe then I'll feel more prepared to handle it all.

Wilson is waiting at the front door, so that I won't have to knock or ring the bell and wake up his parents. I hug him and a nervous giggle escapes. "Shhh," he scolds with a twinkle in his eyes. He takes my hand and leads me to a bedroom on the first floor that I've never seen before, one his grandma sleeps in when she visits. Yellow light from an old lamp on a dresser casts ominous shadows on the wall and illuminates the large bed. Awkwardly, Wilson removes a patchwork quilt from the foot of the bed, worried we'll mess it up, and places it on a wicker rocking chair near the dresser. We look at each other and giggle nervously. Wilson places a finger to his lips, reminding me to be quiet. He walks toward me and holds me, and something in me feels like crying. I don't know whether it's his kindness, or my fear, or an overwhelming sense of carelessness about my life—that cancer has already taken so much, so who cares what I do with the rest?

We lie down on the bed and begin kissing. It all feels a bit forced, like we both know what's coming and just want to just get on with it. Clothes come off and I shiver, longing to crawl beneath the sheets but worried I'll stain them. Wilson reaches under the mattress and produces a Lifestyles condom, and I fear they aren't as safe as Trojan, the only brand I've heard of before. Why do we have to use the free condoms from the freaking health center? Couldn't he have gone to CVS? Wasn't I worth it?

My racing thoughts are cut off as I watch Wilson put it on, astounded. I can't believe this is really happening. *I love him*, I remind myself. *We love each other and this is OK.*

"Is this OK?" he asks, reading my mind. I realize how nervous he is, too, and it makes me feel more relaxed. I nod and put my arms around him and kiss him deeply, willing it to start, willing it to be over.

It's how I imagine most first times must be. Beautiful and clumsy. Good and bad. Hot and painful. Strange and intimate.

Eventually we've both had enough. He pulls off the condom, and we lie in each other's arms. "I'm glad it was with you," he says. I agree and snuggle closer. I'm mostly glad it's over so the cuddling can begin. Maybe that's all I really wanted.

Marisa / Sally

I still can't believe my little Missy is no longer a virgin. I didn't pry, I swear. I just had a hunch—call it motherly intuition. So during one of our late-night chats over her winter break, me lying on Missy's bed, Missy sitting on her pink carpet, I casually brought up my own experiences, saying that sex was different with each partner and usually got better with practice.

"Of course, it's hard when both of you are virgins," I added, looking at her with curiosity.

"Yeah," Missy agreed with a sheepish grin.

"Yeah?!" I asked, raising my eyebrows and smiling.

"Yeah," Missy confirmed, blushing.

"With Wilson?"

"No, with Brad Pitt. Yes, with Wilson! But not until recently—just a few days ago, actually."

"Oh, Missy! Wow! How was it?"

Missy shrugged, embarrased. "I don't know…OK, I guess."

"It'll get better," I promised, laughing.

"Mom! Don't laugh at me," she laughed back.

"I'm not!" I said, but we couldn't stop laughing.

"I can't believe I just told you," she said.

"I know," I said. "I'm glad you did."

"Me, too."

The month with her goes by too quickly. Especially with Missy becoming so much more of an adult, I feel our friendship deepening, our conversations growing more mature. My little girl is growing up.

Finally, the day comes for Missy to go back to school. Jordan's friend who goes to Syracuse picks her up at the house, and as soon as they drive away, I miss her. She is such a beautiful person—both inside and out, and I'm privileged to be her mother. And what talent she has. Over break, she shared with me me all the articles she's written for Syracuse University's newspaper, *The Daily Orange*, and told me about the shows she's been playing with her new band. I'm so proud of her.

To distract myself from missing Missy, I curl up in bed and watch *Prince of Tides*. I love this movie. Nick Nolte has a twin sister in the movie whom he loves very much, and I suddenly wish he were my twin. Someone I could share this awful disease with. The pain and the fear and the hurt. Someone who could get inside my body and share my heartache. It's so lonely to be sick.

Fortunately, I have a consolation prize: Bill will retire next month. Dr. Bruckner even wrote a letter to the NYC Board of Education, persuading them that Bill's support was vital to my recovery—not just the logistics of taking me to treatments and caring for me at home, but his love and compassion. Although both our retirements have come much earlier than we had anticipated, I'm so thankful we'll be able to spend this time together.

Grateful that I'll soon have my Billy home with me each day, I decide to stop feeling sorry for myself. I say a little prayer for Missy at school. And then I sink into my pillows and turn my attention back to the movie.

CHAPTER 18
Angels

Marisa / Sally

Back at school I'm met with silence from Wilson. No calls. No e-mails. Online we exchange a few sparse messages—*hi, what's up*—before the conversation dries up, as if there's nothing left to say. Other times I stare at his screen name, daring him to message me, heart sinking when he suddenly signs off without even a hello.

I instantly regret having had sex with him, realizing we should have done it while we were in love, not as an afterthought. My only solace is that he was my first love, and in the end it was with someone I trusted and loved. I know I don't really regret it, that I'm just hurt and sad it's the end. A few weeks later, we message a bit more and agree, reluctantly, that in order to truly get over each other, we should probably stop talking for a while. We've broken up before, but in my heart I know this is final. I cry more for the "us" I always wanted to be, the "us" that we'll never become. But it also feels right, and a small sense of freedom washes over me.

Added to that is a sense of adventure and excitement, when I quickly realize that Chris is eager to take Wilson's place. Spring semester's Spanish class includes not only him, but Katie and Fern, the other friends I've made on my dorm floor. In class we play Spanish Jeopardy, translate Shakira's Spanish songs into English, put on skits, and make silly videos. College Spanish feels more like kindergarten. Except, of course, I didn't have any crushes like this back then.

He comes to visit me while I'm working at the campus bookstore one Saturday night, where I rang him up last semester, blushing the entire time. He fiddles with the stapler, the tape dispenser, my receipt paper...anything to annoy me. It feels so much like a grade school crush I'm surprised he doesn't pull my ponytail. I finally shoo him away, but when he leaves, I'm still smiling.

He gets my screen name and begins messaging me online. Like everyone, we're more honest there, confessing our crushes on one another. I tell him I'm not ready yet, that I'm getting over the breakup with Wilson. He says he's scared that I'll never get over him. I tell him I'm scared of that, too, but I'm trying.

He meets me and Linda and Katie and Fern at the gym one night, kicking soccer balls and hitting volleyballs and goofing around. He throws his arm around me a couple times, and we all laugh at how he towers over me. The more we giggle, the more he hams it up with hair tousles and pretend headlocks. I can't stop laughing, but I keep my eyes glued to the polished gymnasium floor, too embarrassingly happy to look anyone in the eye.

We bump into him at a house party. "Paco!" my friends scream when they see him. I smile shyly, thrilled to be with him outside of Spanish class, tipsy on keg beer and lust. Hanging out in some stranger's kitchen—him leaning casually against the counter, me standing inches away from him—his hands circle my waist, then pull away. My body aches each time he lets go.

"What?" I ask coyly, looking up at him, begging him with my eyes to come closer.

"I'm just afraid," he says softly, hunching over until his voice tickles my ear. "Afraid you'll run away. Afraid you'll run back to Wilson."

"I don't want to run anymore," I confide. The party's music and laughter disappear into the background, and it's just me and him, and the force of us feels more powerful than the world and my worries and all that we're up against.

Sighing with relief, Chris draws me toward him and locks me in his firm embrace. I breathe, the kind of deep inhales and exhales that make you realize you've been holding your breath for weeks, months, maybe for the whole past year since Mom was diagnosed. I bury my nose in his neck, inhaling the boyish scent of his Irish Spring soap, and run my fingers along his broad shoulders. For the first time at school I feel safe and able to shed my secrets. I stand on tiptoe and whisper in his ear. "Do you want to know why I'm sad all the time?"

I feel him nod, his hand stroking my back.

"My mom's sick," I say miserably, and for the first time the tears running down my face feel ice cold, as if they've grown so used to my story that they're stoic and emotionless. His face contorts, his clenched jaw a mix of anguish and anger on my behalf. Different than Wilson or Tony or Laura, he isn't just observing my grief, it's like he's crawled inside of me so he can see and feel and taste and truly share my pain. He holds me even tighter for what feels like forever, until my friends begin heckling us, and then we laugh and rejoin the party.

Marisa / **Sally**

I call her my angel. Her name is Jennifer, and she's Dr. Bruckner's physician's assistant, an incredibly intelligent and beautiful person. I smile as she walks into my hospital room; I always look forward to seeing her. She's newly engaged, so I'm often admiring her ring and chatting with her about wedding plans.

But today she's not here for chitchat; she's here to give me the results from my latest CAT scan and tumor markers, since I'm at St. Luke's-Roosevelt for another round of chemo.

The tumor in my pancreas has shrunk significantly, she says. However—she saw clearly three spots on my liver.

How depressed I feel from the results. Missy and Jordan race to the front of my mind, their young faces scarred by the worry I've caused them. "I don't want to die," I cry to Bill. He holds my hand and says let's wait to talk to the doctor, but he looks nervous.

Dr. Bruckner comes to see me in the evening. He tells me he's very hopeful for me. The fact that the tumor in my pancreas responded so well to the chemo puts me ahead of the game, he says. So if he's hopeful, I'm hopeful. I've hitched my star to his wagon, wherever it takes me. He stays another ten minutes, popping open my can of soda and drinking it while he watches *Ally McBeal* with me. "I have special tricks up my sleeve for you," he says on his way out. This, after admitting he's had eleven new admits today and is exhausted. What a guy; I like and trust him so much.

My spirits are lifted until I end up having to stay at the hospital until 1:30 a.m. Really an awfully frustrating situation, but necessary to let the medicine get into my body more slowly so that the side effects—nausea, mouth sores, etc.—won't affect me so badly.

Luckily, I'm under the terrific care of two nurses, both named Irene, who are the sweetest people. One works the day shift, the other the night. So, of course, I agree when Nighttime Irene asks me to try Dr. Bruckner's new mouthwash, saying it's good to prevent mouth sores. I take a swig.

"Uch!" I spit it out as fast as I can, then have a funny thought. "Will I end up talking like this… 'Hi, I'm Dr. Bruckner,'" I imitate in his hoarse, *Godfather*-like voice. Irene laughs and calls in another nurse to listen. I have them both in hysterics.

Everyone needs to laugh once in a while, even if it's at the expense of a really lovely and wonderful doctor like Dr. Bruckner.

CHAPTER 19

New England

Marisa / Sally

The spring semester passes quickly. Without Wilson, I'm able to fully immerse myself in college life, and it's a semester of deepening friendships—with Linda, Katie, and the girls on my dorm floor, and with Chris, too. We both know there's something more between us, but becoming friends first feels special, like we both know it's the foundation upon which our romance will rest.

The only thing that spins me out of the Syracuse bubble are the calls from my mom. When the phone rings at midnight, I relax into the everyday chitchat, comforted by how our friendship has resumed and even grown. From the smile on my face, dormmates who pass by in the hall must think I'm talking to a best friend or a boyfriend. Sometimes I laugh extra loud, hoping to fool them further. Even Mom's friendship feels like a secret I must keep, since it's hard to explain our closeness without revealing her illness. Most college kids want to shed their parents; I'm clinging to mine. But my friends are so sure their parents will be home to greet them on summer break, or in four years when they graduate. I have no idea if my mom will even be there when I wake up tomorrow. And each time we hang up, I try to quiet the nagging feeling that Mom's not telling me how she's really doing.

I get a glimpse for myself in May, when school lets out for the summer. As soon as I'm home, we pile into the car and head to Rhode Island for my brother's college graduation. No one thought he'd graduate in four years, but just like with his reaction to Mom's illness, he's suddenly the guy who comes through. I can tell Mom's tired, but she's so happy to be there that she smiles through every family dinner and sobs through the ceremony. Feigning her old level of enthusiasm is a fight, and I wonder if Mom will make it to my graduation, too, which still seems so far away and full of what ifs.

After my first year away from home, being together at Jordan's graduation feels like a family reunion. Even my brother seems different, eagerly introducing me to his roommates and friends as everyone gathers back at his off-campus house near the water. "This is my sister," he tells them, and I love belonging to him in that way, as he proudly tells them I go to Syracuse and that I want to be a writer. I can't believe that in a year he's become my equal, just two college kids reuniting with their parents. But I can tell his friends all know about Mom by her hushed conversations with them in the backyard, and the way they touch her arm as she's speaking and hug her warmly when we say goodbye.

Jordan returns home a week later, but when he opens the front door a tornado rips through the house. She's a tan-and-white blur with a jangly collar and paw nails that click like a typewriter as she runs up and down the stairs. "Sadie!" I exclaim, as she bolts into my room and jumps up onto my bed, knocking me over as she licks my face. But when she trots upstairs to Mom's room, she hops onto the bed gingerly and instantly becomes a lap dog, resting her soft head on Mom's abdomen and staring soulfully into her eyes. My brother adopted Sadie recently and brought her home on a few visits last semester, but this time it's for good. We've had fish and frogs our whole lives, and it feels like we're suddenly living inside a children's book called *The Bardachs Get a Dog!* A pit bull, no less. But no one can deny the tremendous joy Sadie brings, uniting and comforting a family who so desperately needs it.

When I'm not cuddling Sadie, I'm at my summer job selling ice cream on the Long Beach boardwalk. Just one of those girls in the turquoise T-shirts doling out Chipwiches and Flintstones Push-Up Pops to families. I hustle on weekends when the beach is packed, but weekdays are languid and peaceful, with few customers. Facing my plastic chair toward the ocean, I read books my mom has recently devoured and passed on to me. Self-help books like *I'd Rather Laugh: How to Be Happy Even When Life Has Other Plans for You* by Linda Richman, Mike Myer's real-life mother-in-law who inspired his famous *Saturday Night Live* skit "Coffee Talk." We loved the skit so much that when I was younger, Mom would wake me up to watch it. In real life, Linda's twenty-nine-year-old son died in a car accident, and in her fiesty way she shares tips on grieving, my favorite being to let yourself stay in bed all day and watch sad movies (with a list of recommended tearjerkers). Another favorite Mom shares is *God Said, 'Ha!'* by Julia Sweeney, an *SNL* cast member, about her brother's diagnosis of terminal cancer and her own struggle with cervical cancer (my family loves *SNL* almost as much as *Seinfeld*).

Customers can't understand my reading selections. "You're so young! What are you doing reading that nonsense?" one mom says. "Whoa, a bit heavy for the summer, huh?" a dad chuckles. I just give a little laugh and say I like the messages of the books, enjoying a brief moment of believing I can be who they see: a happy college girl with a ponytail serving ice cream. Just once I'd like to reply, "Well, my mom has Stage 4 pancreatic cancer," and watch their jaws hit the boardwalk. Instead, I continue keeping my secret.

I take a weekend off to travel to Massachusetts with my parents to visit my cousins Jeff and Debbie and their beautiful baby girl, Jamie. But I have bigger plans, too. Chris lives outside Providence,

Rhode Island, not far from their house. We couldn't see each other during Jordan's graduation weekend, but this time we make plans to hang out on Saturday night. I tell Mom he's just a friend, and she says, "Uh huh," like she doesn't believe me, not even for a second.

When we arrive on Saturday afternoon, Mom's face lights up at the sight of her great-niece, Jamie, whose big blue eyes scan us skeptically. "Come see your Aunt Sally!" Mom sings out, plopping down on the couch and opening her arms. Nearly two, Jamie hides her rosy cheeks in Debbie's blouse, despite my mom's relentless efforts to draw her out. Finally, late in the afternoon, Jamie shyly starts to play show and tell, walking wobbly across the living room to select a stuffed animal and then place it in my mom's lap. Mom beams and grabs her in a hug while they pose for a photo.

When nighttime rolls around, I put on a retro Strawberry Shortcake T-shirt and my favorite jeans and some lip gloss. I peek out Jeff and Debbie's big bay window every few minutes, waiting for Chris to pick me up. Trying not to seem overeager. Biting my nails, heart racing. *What if we don't even like each other anymore?*

Pacing around the foyer of their house, I hear voices rise and fall around the kitchen table as my parents and cousins close up the Chinese food containers and silverware clangs in the sink. Jeff and Debbie ask Mom how she's feeling, what the doctors are saying. Jamie is sound asleep upstairs, and I long to be like her, away from the inevitable cancer conversation.

Headlights appear. "Bye!" I call. A flurry of "Bye, Missy!" and "Be safe!" echo after me as I gently close the front door behind me, patting my LeSportsac bag to feel for the house key they've let me borrow.

My heart pounds as I walk in the darkness toward Chris's car. A motion-sensor light turns on suddenly from above the garage, and I'm relieved to see he drives a small, beat-up car like Wilson. The familiarity of it calms me. I open the door, sit down, and turn to look at him.

That grin. *Oh God, I'm in trouble.*

I grin back and we both hold it a beat too long. Like the way he used to catch me gazing at him across the room in Spanish class. I look away, embarrassed.

"So, that's it, huh?" Chris teases me. "No hug?"

I smile, feeling myself blush, and then wiggle across the seat and into his embrace. I breathe in his Irish Spring scent, and part of me wishes we could just stay in the car like this the whole night.

Separating, we talk about my cousins and his family as he drives toward his house. I'm nervous. *Will his mom be home? Will she like me? Will it be awkward?* When we walk in, I'm relieved that, like his car, his house is dimly lit and small, with faded blue carpeting and outdated wallpaper. Both seem to match his look of worn jeans, free T-shirts bearing credit card logos, and shabby sneakers. I long to be one of those things, too, something he keeps forever.

Bending down to pet his cat, a fat tabby, I don't even realize his mom is walking down the hall until she's practically in front of me. "Oh, hi!" I say, startled. Willowy and blond, she gives me a weak handshake and a soft hello, but when she smiles she has Chris's same toothy grin. She leaves us and seems to float back to her bedroom. I know his parents are divorced, a messy ending that's left him with complicated feelings about his dad, and I wonder if she's worked hard to stay so pretty and thin, or if she's just naturally that way.

The cat's yellow eyes follow his mom back to her bedroom, but he decides to chaperone us instead. Chris dangles a felt mouse on a long string, swirling the string in a circle to make the cat do a backflip. I giggle, relieved to have an activity to distract us and help us relax. Feigning interest in the cat circus, I study the handsome ringleader… tall, lean and muscular, dark eyes that change from clear to stormy depending on his mood, a sadness to his cheekbones set so high and hollow beneath. Like the poster back in his campus bedroom, Chris reminds me of *The Old Guitarist* from Picasso's blue period, a street musician gaunt and sorrowful playing on the streets of Spain. Sometimes I think Chris sees his own sadness in that musician's face, and that it's more than a poster, but a portrait of sorts.

It's that sadness in Chris's face that I love the most. Whenever I panicked during Spanish class, wondering if I was doing everything wrong by being at school while my mom could die any minute, I'd look over at his face. The curves of his cheekbones seemed fit to carry my flood of tears, and I'd think, maybe I am meant to be here.

After a couple hours of just talking and joking around, he drives me back to my cousins' house and mentions that Jimmy Eat World, our favorite band, is playing in New York City in early September. We could take the Greyhound bus there and back from Syracuse, he says, five hours each way. Do I want to go?

My parents are never gonna go for this, I think. "Sure," I say.

"Awesome," he says, and the grin follows. "I'll get tickets."

He pulls into the driveway, then puts the car in park. We look at each other for a long time, grinning. An electricity fills the car, a chemistry I never felt with Wilson despite liking him so much, a powerful feeling like my whole life could change. Chris tried to kiss me once before last semester and I darted out of the way, still not over Wilson, still not ready to move on. Tonight I wonder if he'll try again. I wonder if I'll let him.

He reaches out for a hug, and I nestle in again, thinking it's safer this way, that the kiss might make me run away again like last time. But secretly hoping: *maybe next time*.

Marisa / **Sally**

On the car ride home from Massachusetts, my morale is boosted from so much time with Bill and Missy, and from seeing my dear nephew and his sweet wife and my adorable great-niece Jamie—with those big blue eyes and dark lashes and hair. I can't get enough of her, yet the morbid side of me wonders if she'll even remember me. She's barely two.

From the vanity mirror, I catch a glimpse of Missy in the backseat, and she seems reenergized, too, though I can't tell whether it's because of family time or Chris. *Just friends*, pshh. What does she think, I was born yesterday? As if I was never young and in love?

We pass through Rhode Island, and I think back to Jordan's college graduation last month. How proud I was to sit in the stands and watch him earn his diploma—and I mean earn. Jordan's never been the best student, but despite struggling with his studies (and multiple threats from Bill and me to stop paying his tuition), he did manage to graduate in four years—and with a business degree. No easy feat, for sure. Selfishly, I'm relieved because if he'd needed another semester or another year, who knows if I would make it to his graduation? Even last month it was challenging just to walk through campus to get from the main graduation to the business school graduation. Drained by chemo, my energy is not what it used to be. Yet everything I am able to accomplish is a gift because I didn't think I would live to see any of this.

I know Jordan's relieved school is over, too, not just because it was such a chore for him, but because it means he can be back home with me. Just like when I was first diagnosed, he's my constant protector, calling me each day from his job in the city at VH1, and checking on me constantly once he returns home at the end of the day. Though he needn't worry, since his pit bull Sadie keeps vigil by my side all day while he's gone. The familiar signs for various towns in Rhode Island blur by, and I bid them farewell, already nostalgic for the family visits to see Jordan we'll no longer have: driving around to see the mansions along the water; eating dinner at our favorite restaurant, Quattro Italian Grille; gobbling up Rhode Island's specialty of fried calamari with hot cherry peppers. But how sad can I be when God allowed me to see my son graduate and let me bear witness to a special day I didn't think I would make?

Driving through New Haven, Connecticut, I make Bill exit the highway so I can show Missy my childhood home. I gasp as we slowly pass the house. My once pristine three-story home is now run-down, with dirty white, shingled siding. Dozens of Orthodox Jewish boys swarm the porch, wearing the traditional tall black hats and *payos*, the curly tendrils that frame their young faces. Shocked, we realize my childhood home has been converted into a *yeshiva*— a school for Orthodox Jewish children. It barely resembles the home I grew up in, where my brothers chased me around the house and then out into the street to play stickball before dinner.

"We can go now," I tell Bill after gaping for a while. He merges back onto the highway, and despite feeling rattled by my childhood house changing so drastically, I remember my childhood fondly. Born and bred as die-hard fans of the New York Yankees, my family worshipped Babe Ruth. Today I think of Lou Gehrig. Upon retiring due to his terrible diagnosis with ALS, he addressed the crowd at Yankee Stadium with this famous statement: "Today I consider myself the luckiest man on the face of the earth."

Lou had no odds to survive—to live. I have cancer and the odds aren't great for survival, but there are odds. That means there is hope. And I will never give up that hope. Because I am the luckiest woman on the face of the earth. I have Billy and Jordan and Marisa, and I love them all so much it hurts. I don't want to be a memory in their minds and hearts—I want to be here.

If you're hit by a car or die of an instant heart attack, you don't get a chance to say goodbye. To express all the love you have for everyone special in your life. But you also don't have all the sadness of letting go. With cancer you die a thousand deaths and it's so emotionally painful.

But if I survive—and I will—it will be worth it. At least I have a chance and I'll fight for that chance to live.

CHAPTER 20

NYC

Marisa / Sally

W e're singing along to every song, gazing up at Jimmy Eat World from the standing-room-only floor of the Bowery Ballroom in New York City. Everything about today has felt magical. Cutting class and sneaking away from campus. Sitting side by side on the bus and sharing headphones to listen to our favorite bands. Squeezing hands as New York City appeared, squinting to see the skyline through the bright setting sun.

Now, sweating in the hot ballroom, I find it hard to remember how freezing it was in Syracuse when I'd listen to these songs last winter. Headphones tucked under my red fuzzy earmuffs, I'd walked along the quad and daydreamed of the Broadway version of the lyrics, with me dancing and twirling through the waist-high snowdrifts. The mix of the music and the giant snowflakes falling had seemed like a snow globe come to life. Smiling to myself on the way to class, I'd felt so grateful to be far away from my gossipy hometown, thankful I'd graduated high school before the news about my mom had leaked out. Back home my secrets felt ugly. At Syracuse, anonymous among twenty thousand students, my secrets feel sacred and beautiful and mine.

Recognizing the intro to each song—whether a guitar strum or a xylophone ding—Chris and I grab each other's arms, so excited to hear our favorite songs live. It's only been two weeks back at school since summer break, but there's a different chemistry between us, like all the bad past has been erased: all the times he tried and I ran, afraid to let go of Wilson, scared to be with someone new. Finally, we have a chance to start fresh. Nothing has happened, not even a kiss. But there are moments when it feels like love without anything having happened at all.

During a slow song, I lean back against him and his hands wrap around my waist, his chin rests on top of my head. I close my eyes and take a peaceful breath, wondering if I'm dreaming.

Sleepless and happy on the midnight bus ride home, we listen on headphones to a Jimmy Eat World ballad about angels. We've lost all the formalities of the trip in. This time his arm is around me, I'm cuddled into his side, we're feeling each other's every breath and sigh. Talking low so we don't wake the sleeping passengers and peering out at the dark and empty highway, we feel like the only people in the world. We confide in one another like old souls who've known each other their whole lives, or perhaps in another life. He tells me about his dad leaving when he was young; I tell him about my brother hiding guns in his closet and swearing me to secrecy. As I say it, I realize I've never shared this story with anyone.

When the bus finally drops us off at 5 a.m., we take a taxi to his off-campus apartment. It's a wordless decision. I anticipate we might just sleep for a few hours before heading to our Spanish class at 10 a.m. But as soon as we lie down on his twin bed, his lips are on mine. Kissing him is intense and passionate and soulful. Never before has it felt like everything has been said, that there are no words left but kisses. My kisses before were instead of words, because words were too clumsy and difficult to say. Eventually we fall asleep, entangled in each other's arms, delirious and deeply in love.

Five days later, the city where we'd just been singing and swaying is attacked. A friend messages me online: "A plane hit the Twin Towers." I click on the news link and am convinced it's a horrible accident. Turning on my tiny dorm room TV, I watch the news as a second plane hits the second tower, destroying the skyline I've known and loved my whole life. Once I see the second plane hit, it's clear something terrible is happening. I call my parents, who thankfully are home in Long Island and not in the city for chemo, and we're relieved to hear one another's voices, though still shaken.

I walk on autopilot to Spanish class. Our professor, solemn and sympathetic, tells us we can stay or leave. Everyone stays. We watch the news on TV and talk about the people we know in New York City and the times we've visited. I volunteer that I went to the top of the Twin Towers just three weeks ago ago with friends. The more politically-inclined students say the attack was inevitable and list the reasons other countries hate us. Chris, a political science major, reveals he wrote a whole paper about conflicts between the U.S. and the Middle East last semester. I hold my tongue, feeling foolish that I thought everyone loved America, that we had no enemies. Chris holds my hand under the table throughout the class, and I feel grateful we're alive and together.

After class, Chris and I sit on the grassy hill in front of the gothic Hall of Languages, looking out onto the Schine Student Center. Chris lapses into lecture mode, talking about the conflict, and I nod along distractedly. It's a sunny day, and I squint up at the clear blue sky, half-expecting bombs to fall. Everywhere students are on their cell phones calling loved ones in New York City or elsewhere. A girl with Greek letters on the butt of her sweatpants and a nylon Longchamp bag is clutching her phone and crying. I feel oddly envious. She'll be able to mourn publicly and feel connected to the thousands of others who have lost someone today, while I'll still be alone in my grief.

What if I lost my mom this way instead? Would a sudden death be any easier than cancer's slow decline, than the awful waiting game of when and how and where will I be, and what will become of all of us?

I lean against Chris and wait.

Marisa / <u>Sally</u>

"**Q**uick, put on CNN," Jordan yells upstairs to Bill and me.

I fumble for the remote. Jordan doesn't keep up on the news regularly, and I can't imagine why he's watching TV instead of getting ready to leave for work.

Bill and I watch, stunned, as the Twin Towers crumble. I'd watched the towers go up in the '70s from the windows in my West Village apartment, and felt attached to the landmark ever since. The paired buildings formed the skyline that represented my independence from my parents, my life as a single woman in Manhattan, and eventually my marriage to Bill, who moved into my apartment only a few months after we met.

And now the city represents so much more: the hospital and all the doctors and nurses who are keeping me alive. The city is my only hope for survival.

Turning off the news, unable to watch the reoccurring images of the planes hitting the towers, I wipe away my tears and try to distract myself by reading, but it's impossible.

That afternoon, Bill, Jordan, and I drive to a bridge at the far end of our town. From the high vantage point, we can see downtown Manhattan. It's smoldering. Dozens of other cars are parked, too, with everyone exiting in slow motion to stare at the smoke. I wonder why we all needed to come here and see the trauma with our own eyes. It's eerily similar to the way everyone seems to search for signs of my demise: my hair loss, my weight loss or gain, my coloring, my mood. Suddenly, I feel protective of the tower remains. I want to tell everyone to stop staring; it's rude.

CHAPTER 21

Love and Terror

<u>Marisa</u> / Sally

After September 11th, everyone talks about when the other shoe will drop. They watch the news, look up at the sky, eye fellow students suspiciously. I am no longer the only one living in fear. Except I don't think the other shoe will be a terrorist attack; I think it will be my mom.

Calls from my dad slowly replace the ones from my mom. Not much for small talk, he reports Mom's latest blood test results, each worse than the one before. I ask him what it means, and his silence is a shrug. "It's in God's hands, Missy," Dad says quietly, and I know that means it's bad, because he doesn't even believe in God. So either he's so desperate he's become a believer, or he's just saying the things you say to placate your daughter when there's nothing left to say. Either way, it's not a good sign. Later in the semester, Dad calls with news that's even more frightening: he'll need double hernia surgery over my winter break. *No, not you*, I think, not realizing until that moment how dependent I've become upon my dad to just be healthy, normal, here.

Each call sends me running to Chris's apartment. Chris meets me at the bus stop, and my eyes well up as soon as I step off the bus and fall into his embrace. We climb the stairs to his bedroom and lie down on the bed. He holds me until I'm ready to talk, threading his fingers through my hair, stroking my back. I finally tell him the bad blood results and the news about my dad, and he grimaces, hugging me fiercely.

Eventually we trudge downstairs so he can makes us dinner—omelettes, his specialty. I sit on a stool at the kitchen counter as he digs out the pan and spatula from the towering pile of dirty dishes in the sink. He scrubs them furiously (they've been sitting there a while), then begins cooking. I laugh as he shows off for me, flipping the eggs high in the pan, crashing the pan down with a thud. He's reckless and careless and hilarious. I compare this to the "plate method" my dad taught me, slowly shimmying the partially cooked flat egg onto a plate, then turning the plate upside down back onto the pan to cook the other side. What once seemed brilliant now feels babyish and cautious.

We go back upstairs and sit cross-legged on his bed to eat, then pile the dirty plates on his desk. Chris turns on music and we lie back down. Elliott Smith's melancholy voice fills the small room. His songs are intimate and heartbreaking, the kind of music I'd normally listen to by myself if I needed a good cry. With Chris, it's a relief to share my sadness without a beat of self-consciousness, without a measure of wanting to retreat on my own. I trace his hollow cheekbones and smile softly at him.

"It's crazy," Chris says.

"What is?"

"You," he says. "You're always smiling, even when all this bad shit is happening with your mom. I don't know how you do it."

"It's just who I've always been," I say, slowly. "And as hard as all of this is, it'd be even worse if I lost myself...who I am."

"See? That's what I mean. It's crazy how fucking beautiful you are."

Tears pool in my eyes, the way they always do when he says the nicest things in the world. We're silent for few minutes, his fingers stroking my arm rhythmically, nervously. Chris starts to say something else, then stops himself.

"What?" I ask. I've told him so much. I want him to finally tell me something.

He confides that he's been depressed since he can remember, from the time he was a little boy, maybe six or seven. It comes and goes, he says, and it's been better since he met me. But when it comes, he warns, he doesn't want to do anything or see anyone. It's bad. Real bad. I hold him close and shush his worries away, wanting to soothe him. He calls me "Angel" and says I was sent from above to save him.

Later, when I tell my mom, she says, "Missy, why do you always fall for the depressed guys? Is it because you're a little depressed, too…because of me?"

"I don't know," I answer, knowing she'll feel overcome with guilt if she thinks I'm depressed because of her. But I know that's why Chris and I have fallen in love. Two sad souls seeking comfort from the impossible world.

Soon, I'm going to Chris's as many nights as I can during the week, and staying at his place all weekend. I sit on his bed and do my homework while he types a paper on his computer. Or we watch movies like *Life Is Beautiful* and *Good Will Hunting*, tilting the computer monitor so we can see from the bed. We live our whole lives in his bed, and when I'm not there—at class, at band practice, having lunch with my friends—I daydream about being back in bed with him.

Several weeks pass by like this until one Friday night, when he tells me not to come over.

"I just want to be alone," he says, his voice dull and emotionless.

"Are you sure?" I ask. "We could just hang out or watch a movie together. We don't have to talk if you don't want to."

I cringe at my own voice, which sounds desperate and needy. But I no longer have any idea how to be without him.

"When I feel like this, I just want to get fucked up," he says flatly. "And I don't want you to see me like that."

I fight back tears but say nothing, willing my silent treatment to make him change his mind.

"OK, well…bye," he says.

I hang up, shaking with fury. I run to him every time I feel sad. How come he can't run to me? Why is he shutting me out? And now what? He'll get fucked up with his guy friends? And what does "fucked up" even mean? Drinking, obviously, but drugs, too? What if he overdoses? What if he tries to kill himself? I already have one person dying in my life. I can't have two.

He doesn't call all weekend and I'm certain we're breaking up. I sit on Katie's bed and cry. "He's crazy about you, Marisa," she reassures me, her green eyes serious and sincere. I can't bear to tell my mom. I don't want her to think poorly of him, having never even met him.

Wanting to get away from it all, I hang out with the only people who never talk about anything: the guys from my punk band. We play Edward Fortyhands, a forty-ounce beer taped to each hand, not to be removed until you've slugged through both. Knowing I'm a lightweight, they go easy on me, duct-taping twenty-two-ounce Coronas to each of my hands. Going to the bathroom is an Olympic feat, having an itch you can't scratch is torture, and by the end of the night we're drunken idiots giggling at everything.

But my laugh sounds hollow. I keep picturing Chris alone in his bedroom, numb and gazing at his computer, or out getting fucked up with his friends, maybe walking too close to the street and accidentally stepping in front of a car or bus. It's the first time that the intensity I love about him frightens me. I don't know what he's capable of.

Sunday night he messages me online, and I'm shaking as I type:

paco81: hey…

starr714: hi

paco81: how r u?

starr714: fine…

paco81: fine, huh?

starr714: …

paco81: yah, that's
what i thought.
you're pissed.

starr714: fine, i'm pissed.
happy now?

paco81: no, i'm not happy.
i feel like a fucking asshole.
this is exactly what i didn't
want to happen.

starr714: it's a little too late
for that

paco81: I love you, beautiful.
i'm just fucked up.
i'm a fucking mess.

starr714: you love me?

paco81: yes i fucking
LOVE YOU

starr714: so you're not
breaking up
with me?

paco81: oh my god,
that's what you thought?
jesus

starr714: i didn't know
what to think.
you didn't call…

paco81: i know.
i'm a big jerkface

starr714: yeah, but i love
that jerkface

paco81: angel…

                              starr714: i missed that…

paco81: i missed you.
will you just come
over?
please?

                              starr714: leaving now

We have sex for the first time that night, needily clinging to one another, tears falling from his eyes onto my face and swimming with my tears. "Angel," he says, cupping my cheek with his palm, gazing into my eyes. "I'm sorry. I'm so, so fucking sorry." He buries his head in my neck and I hold him, trying to absorb his sorrow and relieve him of it. I've never felt closer to anyone, and I decide this was a threshold we needed to cross, and that next time he'll come to me.

But he continues to shut me out every few weeks, one time even kicking me out of his place at midnight, calling his friend Evan to drive me back to my dorm. I hate him on those weekends, and then forgive him in an instant, feeling in my heart that we are both destined and doomed to be together.

Marisa / Sally

Missy's fallen in love. I know because lately when I call her dorm at midnight, she's not home.

"Hi Sally!" Linda says when I call tonight, then awkwardly, "Um, I think she's at Chris's."

I miss our late-night talks, which now happen more like once a week instead of nightly. But I know it's a positive thing for Missy, that it's part of her acclimating to college life and experiencing the adventure of falling in love.

I'll try her again tomorrow night. Or maybe I'll just wait for her to call me.

Besides, I have plenty on my mind. My blood results have been worsening for weeks, and now Bill has to have a double hernia operation next month. Never a dull moment, I tell my friends when they call.

They say, timidly: "Sally, don't you ask 'Why me?'"

"No," I say, surprised to find I haven't thought this even once since my diagnosis. "I think 'Why *not* me?' Everyone has cancer."

I relay this to Missy when she calls me a few nights later, and I'm even more surprised to learn that she doesn't ask "Why me?" either.

"Maybe it's better that it happened to us," she says slowly, the way she does when she's thinking. "We were already so close. What about the moms and daughters who never got a chance to become friends or who just never got along? It'd be so much worse for them."

"You're right," I say softly. Her insight and maturity never cease to amaze me.

We hang up, feeling thankful for the hand we've been dealt. It's the hand that's brought us back together.

CHAPTER 22
Holidays

Marisa / Sally

When the semester ends, I take a bus to Providence to spend Christmas with Chris and his family. Having never been a lonely Jew on Christmas—I've always celebrated Christmas Eve with Laura's family and Christmas Day with my aunt, uncle, and cousins in Brooklyn—it feels strange to ditch my family. Especially since Mom seems to be getting worse and my time with her is so limited.

But my time with Chris suddenly feels limited, too. Instead of returning to Syracuse together for the spring semester, he's going abroad to Spain. On the outside I'm happy for him; on the inside I'm heartbroken. It feels like I'm constantly fighting for more time with the people I love before they're yanked away. With Chris, it just doesn't make sense. Why would I be given the chance to fall in love and finally have support during my mom's illness, only to have it taken away? Chris meets me at the bus stop, all hugs and grins, and I try to shake off the lonely feeling of abandonment and focus on enjoying the little time we have left together.

The holiday cheer is a helpful distraction. On Christmas Eve we have a Yankee Swap with all of Chris's relatives, the gifts of choice being a Pope calendar (my contribution) and a Santa outfit. Finally, I get a chance to snag the outfit, and everyone chants for me to try it on, laughing merrily as the tiny Jewish girl puts on the enormous pants and holds them out like a Jenny Craig commercial. Chris pulls me toward him and plants a loud kiss on my lips. Everyone hoots and I blush, embarrassed and elated to be that girl who's so obviously loved. I always wondered what it would feel like to be that girl. Now I know. My breath catches and I force a smile through a choked-back sob. Huddled together in my sleeping bag that night, Chris tells me it's the best holiday he's had with his family in years.

The day after Christmas, we travel together to my house in Long Island. The introductions are friendly but awkward. Mom makes her usual off-beat jokes to put everyone at ease. She's wearing makeup and a wig to impress him, so it's hard to know how she really looks or feels. But I can tell she's worn out because she excuses herself to lie down before we head out to a restaurant for dinner, which isn't like her at all, especially when we have a guest.

At night, Mom and Dad take us to Domenico's, our family's favorite Italian restaurant. Chris orders gnocchi. We order the same three dishes every time we come, and we've never heard of gnocchi, so we're fascinated when Chris lets us try the little potato dumplings. Mom asks him about his hometown and his family, but he's shy, warming up only when he can talk about how he fell in love with me. My parents shift uncomfortably in their chairs and smile wanly. I can tell they're skeptical of us, but we're so sure of us that we don't care.

We celebrate New Year's Eve with my friends at Lucky Cheng's, a drag bar in New York City. Laura and Chris have zero connection, and I'm thankful for the drag queens who throw their feather boas around our necks and flirt with Chris, making us all giggle. At midnight, Chris kisses me passionately. "Whoa," I hear my friends say, shocked. "Get a room!" They just don't get it, I think. How could they? They've never been in love, and definitely not like this. We make out by the bar until it's time to leave.

The new year has made me anxious from the time I was sixteen, when my grandfather fell on New Year's Eve and then died ten days later. That was the holiday we stole spiked punch from Hailee's parents' party and drank it while locked in her bathroom. The alcohol only heightened my sadness, and I cried in my friend's bedroom, not wanting the clock to strike midnight. But this year—even with Mom sick, and Dad's surgery, and Chris leaving—I feel hopeful for 2002. I feel loved.

Chris stays at my house for the rest of winter break as we spoon on the couch and watch movies. The public displays of affection seem to shock my parents, who enter the living room and then quickly do an about-face. They don't get it, I think, just like my friends. But I'm surprised by my parents' reaction. I thought that, after Wilson being so quiet and reserved, they'd be happy to see me in an openly loving relationship. Oh well. I just cuddle into Chris more.

My brother Jordan's the only one who doesn't seem to mind. Oblivious to Chris and me wanting privacy, he sits down on the recliner next to the couch one afternoon. "What movie is this?" he asks. "*Cinema Paradiso*," Chris says. "Never heard of it," Jordan replies, reclining the chair and settling in to watch with us. I'm half-flattered, half-annoyed. Jordan and I are a little closer now than we used to be, but even when he calls to check in on me when I'm away at school, it's more in that protective-older-brother way than in a friend way. Today I let him join us, relieved that at least someone seems to appreciate Chris other than me.

Soon the fantasy life with Chris is interrupted, as the moment I've dreaded arrives: my dad's double hernia surgery. Before Mom got sick, Dad was the parent I'd spend five minutes on the phone with, after Mom and I'd been talking for an hour. He'd call me "Monkey," we'd giggle at something, and then hang up. But in the past few months, as the updates on Mom have come more and more from

Dad, we've started talking about other stuff: the midterms I'm study-ing for, my latest music review for *The Daily Orange*, the weather (he always wants a report from "the snow belt"). Whenever I return home, Dad hands me a pile of newspaper clippings he's saved for me, mostly concert and album reviews by *Newsday*'s music reporter Glenn Gamboa (Dad is convinced I should e-mail Gamboa for career advice or an internship, but I'm too shy). So his surgery freaks me out. After The Stuff With My Mom, the thought of something hap-pening to Dad, too, shakes my world in a way that leaves me feeling completely uprooted.

After Dad's whisked away into surgery, Mom, Chris, and I sit in the hospital waiting room, and all the worst-case scenarios fill my head. They've found something else while they're in there. They've given him too much anesthesia (I read somewhere that it could kill you). Or what if something happens to Mom while he's in surgery, or at home afterward but he's too weak to help her? While I worry silently, Mom is her usual chatty self, asking Chris about his major and his classes and why he chose to study in Spain. It's probably the most they've spoken the whole visit. I picture the ad: "Hospital waiting rooms: a place for bonding."

I find myself wishing Jordan were here to make everyone laugh with his morbid, off-color jokes. "Don't let them accidentally drop a Junior Mint in Dad," he joked last night, referencing the *Seinfeld* episode we love, the one we all quote too often now that our lives have become mired in medical drama. But I knew his humor belied his fear of not being able to come with us. His job at VH1 was so new he couldn't take the time off.

Chris and I share headphones and listen to songs to pass the time. Mom reads her book. A few hours later, the doctor emerges and beckons to us. Everything has gone as expected, and we can go see Dad in the recovery room.

"Do you want to come?" I ask Chris, hoping my eyes convey I want him there.

"Sure," he says gingerly. He hesitates before getting up, but I'm so eager to see Dad that I don't give it a second thought.

The recovery room, which sounds so sunny by name, looks more like a morgue. Rows of gurneys display patients in various states of dissaray: IVs and tubes jutting out, monitors beeping, a woman moaning. Through the maze of torture, we find the gurney that holds my dad, who's dressed in a greenish hospital gown, disoriented and just starting to wake up. Mom pets his head and speaks in the sing-song voice she usually reserves for Sadie, "Billy, honey... can you hear me?"

I watch the two of them. The situation is so often reversed these days that sometimes I forget how much Mom takes care of Dad, too. I look over at Chris, hoping he's caught this moment and its meaning. Startled, I let out a small gasp. He's pale and shaking, dark eyes darting all over the room. I'm not sure whether he's going to throw up or pass out.

"Oh dear," Mom coos. "Why don't you wait for us outside, Chris? We'll come meet you there."

"Sorry," Chris chokes before rushing from the room, slamming open the double doors that lead back to the waiting room.

I'm not nearly as sympathetic as Mom, my blood boiling as he storms out. Nice that he can go off to freedom, while we're all stuck here in this illness hellhole. I picture running after him, but I don't know whether I'll scream at him or beg him to take me with him. Secretly, I'm envious of his escape—not just from the recovery room, but also his upcoming semester in Spain. He gets to galavant off to a foreign country while I'm stuck with my dad in a gurney, my sickly mom by his side. I'm only nineteen! This can't be my life. This can't be my life. This can't be my life. And if it is my life, why can't I find a guy strong enough to take it? Is that so much to ask?

My anger simmers as Dad becomes more lucid and we're able to take him home. Chris proves useful at hoisting Dad in and out of bed, something Mom's too weak to do and I'm too small to do—

each of us about one hundred pounds compared to Dad's two hundred. Appreciating Chris's physical strength, I block out the emotional weakness I'd witnessed earlier.

But some of the tension never quite dissipates, and now we have to jump the next hurdle: Chris leaving for Spain. On the night before I drive him to JFK airport, we're both anxious in my bedroom, as he struggles to fit everything into his suitcase. I try to help, which only aggravates him more. "Just stop!" he snaps. Tears fill my eyes. Dad, who has recovered from surgery fairly quickly, sees the commotion as he pads past my room. He knocks lightly and offers to loan Chris a small carry-on, which resolves the issue, though we're still shaken. Afterward Chris and I sit on my bed, trying to recover, neither of us wanting to ruin our last night together.

"I have something for you," he says shyly, reaching into his backpack. Wrapped in *The Daily Orange* newspaper is a journal. *It's the only way I stay sane*, I'd told him a few weeks ago, showing him the last few blank pages of the notebook I'd feverishly scribbled in all semester. With each entry, I'd unknowingly documented the story of how we fell in love. But the generic floral notebook pales in comparison to his. A dusty maroon cover (still my favorite color) dotted with tiny stars (for my middle name, Starr) and, in the center, an angel with porcelain skin and a halo of wavy hair (for the way he calls me "Angel"). Each detail a reflection of all the nooks and crannies only he knows. The journal itself a gift he knows will help save me— from my mom being sick, from him leaving. The downside of being known this well: I don't know what I'll do without him.

"Open it," he urges. I take a breath and turn to the first page:

January 6, 2002 2:26 p.m.
Well here's the day we dreaded for so long. It could be worse I'm sure...I could be off to war, or one of us could be transferring. It feels weird to leave you for so long to do something fun and exciting...it won't be quite the same without you there.

I haven't been able to write a lot to you lately because I feel that I don't even need to say anything. There come so many times where we are on the same page, and neither of us needs to explain a thing.

All I can say is that we will change, and we have no idea how. I just hope, with all my heart, that we change togther and that we're on the same page of this story we've created.

I love you
Chris

Marisa / **Sally**

Christmas Day feels strange without Missy here. The food and laughter and board games are all familiar, but a piece is missing. I know I have to allow her this time, though, especially with Chris leaving soon for Spain. Selfishly, I want my little girl all to myself.

Bill and I spend New Year's Eve with friends, and I think of December 31, 1999, the last New Year's Eve I was healthy (or so I thought). It was the night before the new millennium and everyone was panicking about Y2K. Would all of our electronics fail? Would there be a terrorist attack? Would the world as we knew it simply cease to exist?

The anxiety was contagious (and my back pain wasn't much improved), so a few weeks before New Year's, I convinced Bill that we shouldn't buy tickets to see my other favorite Billy—Billy Joel, who was performing at New York City's Madison Square Garden that night. He agreed, though I could tell he was disappointed. He loves music and lives for going to concerts.

It was Missy who put her foot down. "You guys are being crazy! You *have* to go! It's a once-in-a-lifetime opportunity." Oh to be a teenager again, invincible and on a soapbox. "Besides," she continued, "if the world does explode, it won't matter if you're here or there!"

Her naïve logic and impassioned speech somehow worked. Maybe we wanted to drink from that fountain of youth, to return to the times of being young and impulsive and carefree. Bill snagged two tickets and on New Year's Eve, off we went. I vividly remember the pandemonium of Penn Station, the thrill of Bill grabbing my hand and navigating me through the overwhelming crowds. Once safely in the theater, we stood the entire time, dancing in front of our seats, enchanted by the Piano Man.

Thirteen days later I got my diagnosis. Fate can be tricky that way. I was terrified of the 31st, but it was the unlucky 13th I should have feared. We go through life afraid of so many things. But the things that get us in the end are those we never even expect. The ghosts that slink around behind us and tap us on the shoulder. And just like the victims in a horror movie, by the time you turn around and realize what's about to happen, it's always too late.

This New Year's Eve, Missy and Chris come home close to 2 a.m. and sleep 'til noon the next day. Though I'm happy to have her home, I barely see her. They go to the movies to see *The Royal Tenenbaums*, and rent films like *Cinema Paradiso*, meant just for the two of them to watch. Walking into the living room one afternoon, I find them snuggling on the couch. I quickly microwave my tea and scuttle back upstairs, tiptoeing around my own house.

Seeing how they like movies and wanting to spend time with them, we offer to take them to see *A Beautiful Mind*. It turns out to be an incredibly sad and moving story, not only about a brilliant, schizophrenic man, but also about the steadfast wife who stands by his side. As the credits roll, I see that Missy and Chris are glued to the plush theater seats, staring wide-eyed at the screen. Tears are streaming down his face. I think of his depression, Missy's role in his life. The movie has hit too close to home.

"We'll meet you in the lobby," Missy says, trying to sound adult-like but looking worried.

They emerge a few minutes later, Missy holding his hand steadfastly. "Sorry," he says to us with a self-conscious smile, eyes cast downward.

A week later, after Chris leaves for Spain and I have Missy and our house all to myself, I ask her what happened that night in the theater. She says he broke down crying. He felt sorry for being a burden on her, but was also scared of going to Spain and being without her.

"What did you think of Jennifer Connelly's character in the movie?" I ask her.

"I thought she was amazing," Missy gushes. "How she stayed with him all those years..."

We're quiet for a moment.

"Do you think you could handle a life like that with Chris?" I ask.

She pauses. "I don't know," she says finally.

I tell her it's OK, that she doesn't have to decide anything right now. But that it's something to think about if they're together long term. I want her to know that relationships like this are not easy. Inside a strong wife struggling to support a depressed husband is often a shattered woman.

"*Sex and the City*?" I ask, wanting to change the subject, and realizing the season four premiere is about to begin. We started watching when Missy was in high school, me half-jokingly telling her to close her eyes during the raunchy scenes. It didn't really bother me. My mother had been so reserved that I swore I'd be open with my kids about sex.

"Sure!" Missy chirps now, happily racing downstairs to change into pajamas before the show starts. It's moments like these that I see her at age nine, ten, eleven...surely not nineteen.

CHAPTER 23

Distance

<u>Marisa</u> / Sally

I t's a full five days before Chris calls from Spain, and I'm going out of my mind. Still at home with two weeks until spring semester begins, everything feels lonely and full of despair. I promised to visit Chris over my spring break, so I talk it over with my parents and buy a plane ticket for Spain that leaves March 8. It will be my first time traveling outside the U.S., and when I go the post office for my passport photo it feels like proof—proof that we love each other, proof that this isn't some silly college romance, proof that this is *it*. It, it. The it you look for your whole life and clutch with both fists when you find it. The post office worker hands me the tiny, square photo and I expect to see a sophisticated and worldly woman who will soon fly to see the man she loves. But the girl in the photo looks sleepy and scared, a rumpled teenager who just rolled out of bed, a flicker of insecurity in her eyes. *If we're so in love, why isn't he calling?*

When the phone finally rings, I pick it up in my pink bedroom, expecting the long conversations like Tony and I used to have... except Chris is in Belgium and he's drunk.

"Hi, Angel," he slurs. "Muah."

I'm annoyed. With Wilson, I used to love getting drunken e-mails from him because all the *I miss yous* would leak out, all the feelings he'd hold back when he was sober. But Chris is so open about his feelings that when he's drunk it seems less sincere.

We talk for a few minutes, but his friends are leaving for another bar and he has to go. I wish I liked getting as fucked up as he gets. But I can't see myself getting that out of control. There's so much I keep bottled up that I fear it will all come tumbling out. Then I ask myself, "OK, so what if that happened? What's the big deal?" But it *is* a big deal to me. I've grown so used to hiding everything, keeping myself guarded, not letting anyone see how terrified I am of my mom dying. Well, until Chris. But now that he's gone, I'm back to my old habits, and back to feeling alone.

A few days later it's January 13, two years since my mom's diagnosis, and we're crying on her bed, wondering what's coming next and who to blame for all this. Only a few days until I go back to school, and Dad's emotional, too. "Oh, I'm so sad she's leaving," I overhear him say to Mom while I'm brushing my teeth in the bathroom one night. Just like with Mom's illness, his surgery has brought us closer together, and it's the first time I feel sad to leave both of them.

All break they've told me how thankful they are, how I do so much for them, how special I am. If only they knew how inadequate I feel. Ever since the beginning, since she was diagnosed and I turned my back and looked away, I've never felt good enough. I play the role of the perfect daughter to recover from the huge disappointment I was to them back then. I still feel so guilty, so ashamed. I don't think I'll ever forgive myself for that, even though I know they've forgiven me.

I cry myself to sleep, but the next day I'm back to my shitty teenage self, and every little thing my parents do or say pisses me off. I go to my room and close the door. I just want to have a normal conversation where we don't talk about cancer, hospitals, CAT scans, chemo, pain, depression, blood levels, tumor markers, back pain, stomach pain, should have been dead by now. Part of me craves returning to school just so I can have a break from all this.

But at the same time I'm scared to leave. Will it be the last time I see her? No, it can't be. She's not dying. How do you know? She doesn't look like she's dying. How do you know what dying looks like? A man I saw in the hospital, he looked like he was dying. He was so thin he looked like he was going to evaporate. Mom's lost a lot of weight. Shut up. These are the conversations that go on in my head. Am I going insane?

A few days later, I drive back to school. By the third day of classes I'm already wishing away the semester. Counting down the days not to my trip to Spain in March, but to summer or next semester, whenever Chris and I can be together again for real.

I'm in my dorm room getting ready for class when he calls again, this time from Geneva, Switzerland. "I miss you," he says. He's sober this time, but his voice sounds different. I don't know if it's the international phone connection or if it's just that he's so very far away. We talk about our days, but mine sound so boring compared to his new friends and adventures.

Time has never played such an important role in my life, I think as I speed walk to class, fighting the winter wind. Today passed and it's a relief, yet it's awful to sit here and wish my time away so I can be with Chris, when all I want to do is extend the time I have left with my mom.

Nights without Chris bring awful nightmares. When I wake up, I can only remember fragments. Running away from a party and desperately searching for Chris's apartment. Telling Pat from my band that my mom died while standing in a kitchen with millions of hanging black pots and pans, unstable and about to crush me at any second. An intruder holding my family hostage in my house, then finding out my mom is having an affair with him. Mornings after the nightmares I struggle to get out of bed, often skipping my first class and then racing to make it to my next one.

Worse are the days I don't remember the dreams until mid-morning, gasping as I realize, "Oh God, my mom died last night." I freeze in my tracks, in the middle of the quad, students laughing and rushing past me, as I try to separate dreams from reality. Panicked, I call my mom. She chitchats like everything's fine, but I'm not listening to what she's saying—just acknowledging she's alive. The dreams disturb me for the rest of the day and make me afraid to fall asleep at night. And then I feel like a two-year-old. Why the hell am I having nightmares? I'm nineteen!

Each day I feel like I am running, running, running. Running away from my problems, running from my fears, running out of time, running around like a madwoman from classes to band practice to parties so I don't have time to think, running away from my mom each time she calls, running from decorating my room or buying notebooks because I never know how long I'll stay. Will I get a call tomorrow to pack my bags and come home? If I keep running, can I outrun that call?

Last semester I floated from class to class, propelled by the overwhelming urge to see Chris. Even my worst days held the relief of ending up in his arms. This semester my feet are dragging, boots still planted in last semester's snow. I miss looking into his eyes. I miss all the love I used to see there. I even miss the bad parts—the fights, the depression. I know he still loves me and I still love him, but this loss of contact sometimes makes me feel as if I made it all up. It's as if he doesn't exist.

I'm in my dorm room, lounging in bed on a Saturday afternoon, the next time he calls. His voice is dull and fuzzy behind the dim buzz of the phone connection.

"How are you?" I ask.

"Shitty."

My heart drops; he must be depressed again. "What's wrong?"

"Fuck, I don't know," he sighs after a long pause. "I'm just confused."

"What do you mean, confused?" Confused is not depressed. Confused is…I don't know what. My heart is racing.

"I fucking love you, all right? But we're so far apart. I'm just having some…doubts."

"Doubts?" I squeak. My whole body is trembling.

"I don't know. There's this girl I've kind of been hanging out with…"

I say nothing. Tears leak from the corners of my eyes.

"I'm an asshole, OK?" he says. "Just tell me I'm an asshole."

I don't disagree.

"Fuck, I don't even know why I'm telling you this," he says. "I shouldn't be telling you this."

Tears are falling harder now. "No," I finally say, my voice as flat as his. "If you met someone, I need to know."

"It's not like that," he insists. "Nothing's happened yet…"

I feel sick. That means there were almosts. That means there were times he wanted to. Maybe they've kissed. Maybe they've done more. I can't bring myself to ask.

"Look, I fucking love you," he says. "I do. I just feel messed up about everything. I shouldn't have doubted us. Now that I'm talking to you I feel so much better."

"What? So I'm just supposed to forget what you told me?"

"No, I know you can't, Angel. But I'm just telling you it's stupid and to ignore me."

"Now I'm the one who's confused," I say, the mess of my mom and him swirling together, a tornado that has twisted me around and spit me out.

"I'm sorry, Angel," he says. "Don't be confused. You probably felt fine before I called. Just go back to feeling that way and forget I called."

"It's not that easy," I say, torn between fury and feeling that without him I have no firm footing in the world. "I'll try," I promise weakly.

I hang up and look over at the photos hanging above my bed: the two of us smiling, laughing. Suddenly, last semester feels like a stupid fairytale.

Linda and Abbe, another friend from our dorm, console me that night over Chinese food takeout before heading to a party. They're pissed in the way best friends get, calling him a fucking asshole and offering to go to Spain and throw him in front of running bulls. I laugh, an empty cackle, but it's not bulls I'm picturing. It's torturous scenes of him walking hand in hand with someone else down moonlit streets in Madrid. The almost kisses he had with me freshman year are now the almost kisses he's having with her. I imagine myself approaching them in the street and screaming at him, then sobbing and throwing my arms around his neck when he begs me to take him back. If only I were there, he'd remember what we have…right? Or would he choose her anyway? Is this all just a game he plays? Make a girl believe he's in love with her, torture her with his depression and shut her out, and then do it all over again? Am I just the idiot who fell for it? I shove down the thought with more lo mein.

We head to the fraternity across the street from our dorm for our friend Joe's twentieth birthday. God we're old. I'm happy I'm still nineteen. I think I'll stay here as long as I can. At the party, we hug Joe and our other guy friends, and Pat and Al from my band. We all play beer pong and flip cup and take shots and then my friends disappear. I'm sure they're just off talking to other people, but I suddenly feel desperately alone. I don't want to be anywhere—not home, not school, not here at this party—and I don't want to be with anyone—not my friends, not my band, not even fucking Chris the fucking asshole—and I don't want to be me—a pitiful little girl with a dying mom and an asshole boyfriend.

I lean against a wall and slowly slide down until I reach the sticky floor, sobbing into my arms. The music is so loud it's drowning out my sobs and I can cry as hard as I want. I feel invisible.

Apparently I'm quite visible, because soon Al and Pat are beside me. "Dude," Pat says firmly, their nickname for me, the only girl in the band. "Dude, come on, what's going on?" I just sob and sob.

Al stays with me and pats my shoulder awkwardly while Pat runs off. He comes back with Linda and Abbe.

"Miss!" Linda says, crouching beside me. "Drummer girl! Come on, let's go take a walk."

They hoist me up and I lean against them as we stagger back to the dorm, crying my head off the whole way. Once it's started it seems there's no sign of stopping, and for once I don't feel embarrassed about letting it go.

I wake up at 5:25 a.m. in my bed (I vaguely remember the girls tucking me in). I'm wearing last night's clothes, and my halter top twists against my neck, as if trying to strangle my sobs. I thought I'd wake up renewed. Instead I feel hollowed out. I don't know who I am, or how I, of all people, became the drunk, crying girl at the frat party.

Phone calls with Chris change after that. He grows depressed, the longest bout of it I've witnessed, conversations consisting of him telling me how shitty he feels in that dull, flat voice. I'm worried about him, but I feel very far away from him, and I can't seem to get the old feelings back. I don't feel strong enough anymore to handle his depression on top of my own, which now I can no longer deny.

Ever since I bought my plane ticket in January, I've pictured the scene in the airport. I'll step off the plane and feel that rush as he walks toward me. I'll fall into him and we'll hug and kiss and cry and laugh and walk off together, knowing everything will be OK. It's only a month until I leave, but lately the scene is blurry. I can't picture walking off that plane. I can't even picture getting on.

Marisa / <u>Sally</u>

"Mom, everything's a mess," Missy tells me when I finally get her on the phone. She's been avoiding me for the past two weeks, conveniently "about to head out" each time I call, with empty promises of "I'll call you later." Eager to finally catch up, I adjust my pillows to sit up straighter in bed.

"What happened? What's wrong?" I ask, blinking, trying to rouse myself from the chemo brain fog.

"Oh Mom, everything," she says. "Hang on."

I hear her walking, probably to the hall or the common room where she can get some privacy.

"Hello?" Missy says once she's found a spot.

"Hi, doll, I'm here. Now tell me what's going on. Is it Chris?"

"Yeah," she says miserably. "I don't know. Things just feel off with us."

"What do you mean?"

She hesitates. I sense her contemplating what to share, what not to share.

"He's just so far away. He says he's having doubts..."

"Doubts?"

"Yeah."

"About you?"

"No, Mom, about what to eat for dinner. Yes, about me. About us, really."

"Oh Missy," I say. "What about you? Are you having doubts?"

"No," Missy says defensively. "Well, I don't know. I wasn't until he was."

"Well, that's normal. So where do things stand now?"

"I don't know. After we spoke, he said he felt better. But now I feel worse."

"Do you still want to go visit him?"

"Yes, of course! It's just a fight, Mom," she says, all huffy.

"O-kay," I huff back. "Just asking."

"I know. Sorry," she mumbles.

"It's OK, doll. I know you're stressed. You have a lot on your mind."

"I just wish I could see him," she says. "It would make it so much easier to get back to normal."

"I know. Soon enough, right? Just another month."

"Yeah," she says, but I can tell she's not convinced.

"How's everything else? How's Linda?"

"Ugh, she's mad at me."

"Really? Why?"

"I was supposed to pick her up to go to these parties over the weekend and I kind of...forgot."

"No!"

"Yeah."

"So she was just sitting around waiting for you?"

"Yeah."

"Missy, that's not nice."

"I know, Mom," she says in a testy voice.

"OK! OK! Don't bite my head off."

"Sorry," she mumbles again.

"So what happened?"

"She hasn't spoken to me since. Which is pretty awkward when you live in a freaking shoebox."

"Oh, Missy. Did you apologize?"

"Yeah, but she didn't really care. She's still mad. She's pretty good at holding a grudge."

"Well, I know she values you as a friend. She'll come around."

"I hope so. Anyway, how are you? How are you feeling?"

My eyes flit to the spiral notebook next to me on the bed, open to my latest scrawl. The lousy blood test results, the crappy tumor markers, the added medications, the uncomfortable side effects, and my never-ending list of questions to ask Dr. Bruckner and Jennifer, which all basically boil down to this: how can you save me?

"Oh, pretty good today," I say. The last thing Missy needs to worry about is me.

CHAPTER 24
Breakup

Marisa / Sally

I'm sitting at the airport in Syracuse waiting to fly home to see my family for the weekend. Everyone looks so composed—going on business trips with long black trenchcoats or flying to see loved ones for Valentine's Day. I feel defeated. Lately, I can't even smile at friends when I see them on campus. I try to form some sort of smile only to realize those muscles have simply stopped working. I feel so lost here—lost in Syracuse, lost in a giant list of events, lost in my thoughts. I need to be around my family, people I love who love me, but mostly I need to be reminded of who I am. I just want to sit and talk to my mom about everything.

But when I see Mom, she's tiny and frail and not feeling well, getting up slowly out of the car to hug me hello. Only a year ago she ran to greet me as soon as she spotted me exiting the terminal. But she perks up once we're back home and stays up until 2 a.m. talking to me. I don't hold anything back this time, no longer worried about giving Chris a bad reputation. It's nothing he hasn't brought on himself, I reason. Sitting at the kitchen table, I spill everything: his horrible bouts of depression, the weekends he ignored me, the phone call where he said he was having doubts and met someone else, the pressure of going to see him.

Mom holds my hand and sympathizes with how hard this is on me. That I already have enough to worry about with her, how tough it must be to have this on top of it. For the first time all semester I feel *seen*—as if Mom is able to look back and see a snow globe version of me, tiny and struggling against the Syracuse winter. I was afraid she would badmouth Chris, or act hurt that I didn't tell her the whole truth earlier. Instead, she's just on my side. And even though this is the weakest I've seen my mom, just talking to her makes me feel stronger.

"I wish I knew what to tell you to do," Mom says, "but it's your decision to make."

Mom's words flood me with warmth (finally, she sees that I'm a grown-up in a grown-up relationship!), then panic (are you *sure* I should make this decision by myself?). Sensing my anxiety, she helps me make a plan. She suggests I call Maxine, my aunt who's a psychologist, and also Chris's mom to let her know what's going on. I agree, feeling a sense of purpose—and relief. The need for real grown-ups only emphasizes how much I'm in over my head. Still I resent relying on my mom, or Chris's mom, or my aunt. I spent the previous semester feeling like if I had Chris, I didn't need anyone; it was me and him against the world. But now, without him, I feel reduced to a little girl again, and I'm not sure whether to feel shackled or sheltered by all these adults in my life.

I'm putting our tea mugs in the sink when Mom asks, "Have you thought about canceling your trip to see him?"

"No," I say quickly. But her question stays with me the rest of the night, repeating in my head the way all the important questions in life do, as I sleep fitfully in my childhood bed in my saccharine pink bedroom.

I wake up the next morning to Chris's voice on the answering machine. I catch the end—"I love you"—and the answering machine's beep and time recording: "11:05 a.m." I scramble for the phone, but my needy voice echoes into the receiver: "Chris? Chris? Are you there?" I missed him.

Two minutes later the phone rings again and I pick it up, still half-asleep, expecting it to be Chris calling me back. Instead it's my Aunt Maxine. I start telling her everything, in my sleepy voice that sounds like *The Exorcist*. I ask her about Chris's depression, how to get him to get help. As I describe his symptoms, I hope she'll tell me I'm overreacting. Instead, she sounds concerned—about him, but more so about me.

"Have you thought about getting out of the relationship?" she asks.

I'm devastated. First Mom with canceling the trip, now Maxine with the whole relationship. I want to fight them, tell them they're wrong, but I don't have the strength. Deep down, I know they're both right.

I go upstairs and Mom shifts over so I can lie beside her, my head on her chest like I'm a little girl. I relay what Maxine said as she strokes my hair. I tell Mom I want to be Jennifer Connelly from *A Beautiful Mind*. Even when her depressed husband endangers her and their baby, she stays with him and fights for him. And it's not just a movie—it's based on their relationship in real life. How did she do it? I want to be there for Chris, I want to continue loving him for my whole life, but I don't know if I can.

I return to my room thinking I'll write in my journal, but instead I flip through the pages, trying to understand where things went wrong.

All I can say is that we will change, Chris wrote on the first page before he left for Spain. The line had consumed me. Things were perfect—why did we need to change? Couldn't we just freeze time and pick up right where we left off?

But it wasn't change I should have feared; it was staying the same. Chris continuing to be depressed. Me continuing to feel abandoned by him while anticipating an even greater loss. Spain just put a spotlight on all the things that weren't perfect at all.

And I was partially to blame. Stupidly, I'd tricked myself into believing things were perfect because the dream of it felt so deserved. See? It's OK to lose my mom because I'm in love! And I'll be the girl whose mom died, but I'll have him by my side! And I'll live out my days with someone who knew her and was with me when she died! See, world? It's OK! I'm OK!

But now I don't know if I'll ever be OK. This isn't the way my story is supposed to go. It made sense to gain him and lose her. It made losing her make sense. Because it's been two years since her diagnosis, and I still can't make any sense out of losing her. Throwing my journal across the room, I blast music so Mom can't hear me sob.

The next morning, Mom encourages me to call Chris's mom—a woman I've only met twice, but the only woman other than me who might be able to help him. I'm afraid she'll be flaky, but I'm surprised to find she's strong and determined. She's going to call Chris, she's going to call Chris's doctor, and maybe have Chris come home if that's the right thing for him. She thanks me profusely for letting her know and for being there for him. Call me anytime, she says.

What she doesn't know is that I'm dumping him on her doorstep. I'm dumping him.

Mom helps me make a new plan. That afternoon she takes me to see her allergist, Dr. Lubitz, with his twitchy mustache and dime-size dandruff flakes. Nothing's wrong with me, but I let him examine my nose and ears while he and Mom talk about me as if I'm not there. He's always had a soft spot for Mom, whose two-minute allergy shots turn into hour-long conversations as she listens compassionately to his problems the way I'm sure no other patient does. This visit the tides have turned. Mom explains my situation, and in a heartbeat he scribbles a doctor's note and hands it to me. *My patient, Marisa Bar-dach, cannot fly on March 8 due to severe bronchitis.* Mom thanks him profusely and walks to the car with her shoulders held back in a triumphant pose. She can't cure my heartbreak, but this, this she can do. It reminds me of a TV show I once watched about a mother who, filled with adrenaline, somehow lifted a car to free her trapped baby. I realize now: that's how fiercely my mom loves me. I pause in the parking lot.

"Did you forget something?" Mom asks, looking back toward the allergist's office.

Yes, you, I want to say.

My face crumples and tears soak her shoulder as I hug her in the middle of the parking lot, for once not even caring who sees.

We use the note to refund my plane ticket, and I call Chris to tell him I'm not coming. He's so numb that he barely reacts, only saying in a flat voice: "You know if you don't come it's over."

I return to school heavy-hearted. A week later Chris calls to boast that it's the happiest he's been since he arrived in Spain. His voice is animated. He's making jokes. He agrees all this is for the best. "I finally feel relaxed here, now that I don't have to worry about stuff with us."

What I'd wanted to hear: this is a huge mistake—a giant misunderstanding—and if not now then later on down the road we will be together.

Surely this can't be the end.

I call my mom. "If he's so happy now, what does that say about how he ever felt about me?" She shushes me and counts down until spring break, when I'll come home to Long Island instead of visiting Chris in Spain. "Only two more weeks," she promises.

But home is not a reprieve for my mind. The evening of March 8 comes and all I can think is: *I'm supposed to be on a plane right now.* I close my eyes and imagine squirming on a red-eye, unable to sleep because I'm too excited to dash off the plane and into Chris's arms. I picture sitting with him in a Spanish café and mapping out which tourist attraction we'll see that day because I never even bought a guidebook; the only thing I ever cared about was being with him. This should be the most romantic week of my life, with Spanish flowing off my tongue and my boyfriend unable to keep his hands off me. But when I open my eyes, I'm in my childhood bedroom and it's as if Chris never happened. And I have no idea where—geographically, emotionally—I'm supposed to be.

By the time the flight's scheduled to land—March 9, 1:30 a.m.—I've never hated a country so much in my life. I hate Spain. I hate Chris. And I hate that neither of those statements are true.

Mom tries to comfort me with shopping trips and *Sex and the City* episodes until Dad playfully scolds us, reminding us that she needs her rest. I sulk back to my room, feeling the double loss of her and Chris.

I go back to Syracuse a few days early to record an album with my band. We're in the studio all day, and then I'm in my dorm room getting ready to go out with the guys that night when the phone rings. I'm sure it's Pat or Al bugging me to hurry up, but when I pick up it's Chris. Only his voice sounds like he's been sucking helium— the same way it sounded when he called from Amsterdam drunk. Oh shit, it's 5 a.m. there on a Saturday night. He's definitely drunk.

He barely talks in the beginning, and I'm trying to figure out why he called in the first place. But I'm feeling good from the day: I recorded an album with my band and talked on the phone with Laura, Linda, and my mom (twice). So I ask him bullshit stuff about Spain, spring break, his trip to Ireland. Finally I ask him how he's been feeling about everything.

"Everyone's girlfriends are coming to visit," he says accusingly. "Even quasi-girlfriends and ex-girlfriends."

"Chris," I say, surprised by my firm voice, but feeling strengthened by the support of my mom and my aunt and my friends. "One week in Spain wouldn't have solved our problems. It's more than just the distance. The depression stuff would have come up with or without you being away."

"I disagree," he argues.

"What do you mean?"

"Whatever," he says, his voice clipped and ice cold. "It doesn't matter. I'm still here and you're still there."

"I'm not just gonna sit here and listen to you make me feel bad," I say, finally fed up with his guilt trips. "I just started feeling OK with my decisions."

"Ugh, that's not what I meant. Fuck. Now you just think I'm being a big asshole."

"No, but that's just the tone I'm getting from this whole call."

"Well, how do you want me to feel, Marisa? How do you want me to fucking feel? Tell me."

I say nothing.

"It just sucks," he says, "because I already know how I feel. I'm still fucking in love with you and I don't know what to do. Fuck. And now you just think I'm a fucking asshole to call you up and make you feel bad. I just want to talk to you. Fuck. And you're trying to figure everything out and you don't even know if you're in love with me or not. Fuck. I'm just gonna go…" His voice trails off.

"What? I just—"

"I'm gonna hang up. I'll talk to you some other time."

Click. I bang my phone down, yank open a dresser drawer, and slam it shut so hard it shakes the mirror behind it. Then I go out drinking with the guys.

After that I call my mom nightly. "You only call to cry," she says, lightly teasing, trying to make me laugh through my tears. "You were always so happy. I don't know who Marisa is anymore."

"I don't know who Marisa is either," I reply.

Marisa / **<u>Sally</u>**

Missy, you are so precious to me. I'm grateful you didn't go to Spain and that you said I was so helpful to you. I didn't know because I became so emotionally involved myself. I'm happy I was here for you.

CHAPTER 25
Summer

Marisa / Sally

"Did you know Brooke's mom died?" Laura asks when I pick up the phone in my childhood bedroom.

At this point, I'm used to her not saying hi—only now I see it as a symbol of our friendship. Our distant college lives have brought us closer together over the past year, and lately I even seek out Laura to talk to her about the breakup or my mom. But it's strange to suddenly have another mom to discuss.

I switch the receiver to the other ear, sure I heard her wrong. "What?"

"Shari just told me Brooke's mom died. I think a few weeks ago."

"Are you serious?" I say, panic darting through my veins. Is everyone dying? Is this just what happens now? I've been home for summer break for barely a week, and already, everything's falling apart. I sit on the edge of my bed.

Brooke lives a few towns over and went to travel camp with us back in middle school. We were thirteen and our long bus rides were spent singing Disney songs, pranking our camp counselors, and obsessing over boys. Whenever we went to Brooke's house, her mom always insisted we stay for dinner, making elegant dishes for us that our mothers never made. I remember her once setting out blueberry-and-cheese blintzes with sour cream, the sweet and tart taste still present on my tongue but now in a slightly nauseating way.

"Was she sick?" I ask, my only point of reference for how moms die.

"I don't know. Maybe you should call her, Maris…" she says, in the voice that means I should.

"I know. I will. I definitely will," I say, convincing myself with each word. I do and don't want to know every single detail. I glance into the hallway and upstairs to where my mom rests in her bedroom. It's strange to hear that the moment we've been waiting for has happened to someone else. I try to picture Brooke right this minute in her childhood bedroom, but I can't read her expression. What is it like to be on the other side of grief? Is she stone-faced in mourning? Is she sobbing, devastated? Is she secretly just the tiniest bit relieved it's over? A morbid curiosity consumes me, and I long to step into her shoes for a minute, just to see how it will feel. Suddenly, I realize these are the calls friends will make about me. *Did you hear Marisa's mom died?* The gossip I've avoided will be inevitable then. We will be reduced to town news, not real people who are suffering, who have suffered for so long. I get the sense that only I know what this is really like for Brooke, and I feel a sudden responsibility. I know I have to call her.

"I'm sorry, Maris," Laura says. "I wish I didn't have to tell you, but I knew you'd want to know."

"It's OK," I say dully. "I'm going to go call her. I'll call you back after."

I sit on my bed for a moment, stunned, then dial Brooke's number before I lose my nerve. I listen numbly as she tells me about the suddenness and the shock, how her dad can't deal so she's the one taking care of her younger brother, how she couldn't get out of bed for a week.

"You know what I mean, with your mom and all," she keeps saying, seeking comfort in our shared sorrow. But I want to scream—to her, to Laura—"My mom is still alive!" The news of another mom dying has left me dizzy and disoriented, with Brooke's mom and mine tangled into one, the dead and the dying, two daughters devastated.

I hang up and trudge upstairs to Mom's bedroom, each footstep impossibly heavy. Like Laura with me, I can't bear to tell Mom, but I don't know how not to. I need too much for her to comfort me. Mom's flipping through the TV channels, but looks up when I walk in. She reads my face in a heartbeat. "What's wrong?"

"Brooke's mom died," I say, still stunned.

"Oh, Miss! No…"

"I know."

I lay down beside her and rest my head on Mom's chest, her slender fingers stroking my back. Agitated, I lift my head and put it back down, again and again, trying to find a comfortable position. Mom's bony clavicle pokes at me, an incessant reminder that Brooke's mom dying is a warning sign, and that it's only a matter of time.

"You don't know what to do with yourself," Mom observes, reaching out for me.

"I know," I say miserably. I get up from the bed. All I want is Mom's soothing touch, yet being near her just saddens me more. And I can't bear for her to see me mourn for her when here she is, still living. *It's Brooke's mom who's gone*, I scold myself, but they feel one and the same. A spiral of sorrow.

I trudge back downstairs, footsteps more leaden than before. I sit on my bed in a stupor, tears distorting my pastel room into a watercolor blur. I don't want to call Laura back. I don't want to return Chris's calls or e-mails, the ones I've been avoiding for weeks out of fear that in a moment of weakness I'll take him back. Mom's right: I have no idea what to do with myself.

Marisa / Sally

"Miss!" I call down a few minutes after she leaves my room.

"What?" she calls upstairs, forcing composure when it's obvious she's been crying.

"*You've Got Mail* is on! It just started! Channel 7."

"OK!" I hear the movie echo on her little white TV and picture her lying belly down on her bed to watch.

On the screen, Meg Ryan's just entering the charming little bookstore she owns, unaware that she's about to fall in love with Tom Hanks, who owns the big bookstore that will put her out of business. I pull my brown blanket up to my shoulders and try to calm my breathing. Missy telling me about Brooke's mom has riled me up, and I can't relax. I hope the movie is helping Missy calm down, too.

An hour later, as Meg Ryan is about to shutter her shop, she remembers herself as a little girl, her now deceased mother spinning her around and around the bookstore as if they're in a ballet. I think of my mother and me, me and Missy, the beautiful and inescapable circle of grief. I'm weeping, and I have no doubt that Missy is, too.

CHAPTER 26

Surgery

Marisa / Sally

The phone rings at midnight, like it did in college—except I'm still home on summer break and Mom's in the hospital, drugged up for her surgery tomorrow.

"Missy, let's go to Mexico," she whispers conspiratorially, sounding more like she's in the psych ward than the cancer wing.

"Mom…" I say, half-laughing. Dad warned me she was out of it, but geez.

"I plan to escape," she hisses. "So come get me and we'll go."

"Mom…" I try again, but I don't have the heart to tell her we can't go.

"Life sucks," she says, her voice breaking. "I'm tired of all this."

"Maybe we can go when you feel better," I concede. Anything to make her stop crying.

"OK," she sniffles. "I hate it here."

"I know, Mom," I comfort her. "We'll go to Mexico. We will. You deserve a trip. You've been fighting so hard."

I tell her I love her and say goodnight, worried it's goodbye. Climbing the stairs to Dad's room feels like an Olympic feat. I find him lying on his side of the bed watching David Letterman, Mom's empty side of the bed still neatly tucked in.

"She's threatening to break out of the hospital and go to Mexico," I report. I'm trying to be funny, but it sounds dry and bitter.

"She can't go to Mexico!" Dad exclaims, sitting up in bed.

"No shit."

We exchange looks like prison guards talking about a rogue inmate. *What do we do with this one?*

The teams switched this month, and suddenly it's me and Dad. We've spent the past two weeks in a new rhythm: Dad sits with Mom at the hospital all day; I go numbly to my summer internship and then take the subway to meet them. We sit beside Mom's hospital bed, trying to choke down our dinner without staring at the green gunk that slides down a clear plastic tube that emerges from her hospital gown and empties into a basin by her bedside. "What was that?" Mom asks, when a particularly alarming color passes through: bright green or blood red. For the drive home from New York City to Long Island each night, Dad and I retrieve the car from the parking garage and blast Blink-182, singing jokily to "What's My Age Again?" For a moment we're free of the hospital's fluorescent lights, machine beeps, and strange-colored gunk, and we can pretend we're on a joyride as the city skyline races past. But a few songs later we stare somberly out the front windshield as the opening lyrics of "Adam's Song" echo along the dark highway before us. It's a song about death and loneliness, and, silently, it makes us both petrified of mom dying alone during the rare hours we're not by her side.

I hug Dad goodnight and trudge back downstairs to my room, feeling helpless. I'm on Team Dad in my day to day, but I'm on Team Mom in my heart. If only I could take her to Mexico. She's begging her daughter to help her, and there's nothing I can do.

It all started two weeks ago. We were in Connecticut visiting Aunt Sherry and Uncle Stuart, and Mom was sick all weekend. We knew it was bad when we were out to dinner at Mom's favorite Chinese restaurant and she spent the whole time in the bathroom throwing up. It continued all weekend, but Mom insisted on not cutting our trip short. She loved being in her home state with her older brother and sister-in-law. Their colonial house, wrapped in '50s farm motif wallpaper and surrounded by dense woods, has been a safe haven for our family for as long as I can remember.

We probably should have left sooner. The moment we got home, Dad and I brought her to the emergency room. After several days of tests and poking and prodding, the doctors told us that the pancreatic tumor had grown and was pressing on the passageway that allows food to travel from the stomach to the small intestine. In short, there was a blockage. The only option was surgery to create a different passageway from the stomach to the small intestine.

"We just need to reroute traffic from Fifth Avenue to Park Avenue," one doctor joked.

It sounded crazy to me. But not to the patient.

"It's this or perish," Mom said drowsily, agreeing to do the surgery.

Lying in my bed tonight, I try praying to God, but I don't know what to wish for. I'm afraid of losing her, but equally afraid of her surviving the surgery and continuing to live a miserable existence of pain, hospitals, suffering, and fear. I mourn the life I envisioned for her—retiring to Florida, playing golf with Dad in the sunshine, old age. I grieve for my kids not having a grandma. I feel cheated of the most simple wish.

Finally, I decide what to pray for: just don't let her die in a hospital—in a place she hates. Let her die at home, in the house she adores, with the family she loves. And then, if it's time for her to go to a more peaceful place, I may be able to accept that. Maybe.

My prayers work. A week later Mom comes home from the hospital. "A Father's Day treat," Mom says, all of us thankful to be together as a family for the holiday. I give Dad a book on The Who's *Tommy*, the first Broadway show we all saw together as a family, and find a Neil Young biography for my mom to give to him. I'm determined it won't be a failure of a Father's Day. Dad needs to know we haven't forgotten about him. *If she leaves us, you need to stay*, I tell him in my head as he hugs us for his gifts, squeezing me extra hard because he knows I bought both.

Once home, Mom returns to sleeping in my bed, where she's been more comfortable since being sick. I set up an air mattress on the floor and sleep next to her. I'm relieved to have her home, but it feels like only part of her has returned, like she's in some faraway place between life and death. Pain, fear, and insomnia plague her. How much longer will she really keep fighting to live?

"Who ever thought I'd end up like this?" she repeats all the time to no one in particular, not expecting an answer. Her once-animated voice is now slow and lethargic, as if she's talking in her sleep. I just touch her arm or hug her.

When I'm not sleeping beside her or caring for her, I race between two jobs—my first internship at a national magazine in New York City, and a part-time job at Häagen Dazs in my neighborhood. I love and hate the escape, wondering if I'll later regret spending my time sending magazine mailers or scooping ice cream instead of being with my mom.

At night, I can only sleep if I picture Chris's arms around me, even as I dodge his e-mails and phone calls. I still love him desperately. But looking over at Mom, finally asleep and as still as the dead, I know I can't ask for any more drama or hurt than I already have.

Marisa / **Sally**

I don't know when this started or how I got this way, but I feel it's a dirty trick. I tell Maxine, Bill's cousin who is a breast cancer survivor and a psychologist, "I feel closer to death now than I do to life."

I have to fight these feelings. People are coming to see me in the hospital tonight, and I don't want to keep breaking down.

It seems the pancreatic tumor got larger and is pressing against the smaller intestine. It causes me to throw up and I can't digest my food. So they have to feed me through a tube.

I don't see how I'll ever bounce back, but I really must. I want to spend time with my children and give them what I can. I want to love my husband to pieces because I'll never be able to get along without him—even for a few minutes—and I'm at a loss. How does he do what he does? Does he cry in the dark by himself? Does he really have that much confidence in me pulling through this episode? It's so hard to see a positive outcome anymore.

I call my neighbor Barbara to tell her I'm in the hospital. She says, "Sally, are you in pain?" I reply, "It only hurts when I cry."

CHAPTER 27

Go Go Go

Marisa / Sally

Three days ago—July 14—I turned twenty, and it feels like the rubber band inside my mind has snapped. Squinting against the sun shining in through my pink shades, I glare at my alarm clock and yank my flowered comforter over my head. So much for the girl who woke up giggling. Today all I can do is sleep until 3:30 p.m. and skip my magazine internship because I'm scared to face the world.

My mom called me at my internship yesterday, her voice slow and hazy and pained, and I realized something: she is not getting better and this is not going away. After she recovered from the surgery, I tried ignoring the truth. Friends would ask, "Oh, so she's better now?" and, tempted to agree, I'd nod my head yes, knowing that the real answer was no.

But this is going to continue and worsen, I realize each morning when I wake up. And I dread it in the pit of my stomach. I dread it on the top of my throat where the tears form. I dread it as I sob in the bathroom stall at my internship, shoving a fist into my mouth so my colleagues can't hear.

Tossing in bed, not even bothering to get up and eat breakfast or lunch or whatever meal makes sense at 3:30 p.m., I debate calling Laura or Shari, but my friends seem so far away. Everyone else seems to be having blissful summers—camp jobs, new friends—and suddenly I hate talking to them. I am so changed. I try to think of anything positive to say about my spring semester, about my summer, and I come up with nothing.

My mom is home from the hospital and I'm supposed to feel better and hopeful and *I can't! I can't! I can't!*

Mom must hear my movements because she comes in to check on me, sitting on the edge of my bed and smoothing my hair. She asks if I want to see a therapist. It's instant déjà vu of that awful fight two-and-a-half years ago. I feel backward, like I'm seventeen again instead of twenty, but I agree to go. Thank God for Mom, who always sees through me. She finds someone new and books me an appointment.

I cry while I'm driving to see the therapist, blasting Bright Eyes "The Center of the World," the singer's voice a shaky sob that mimics my own. I cry in the therapist's office as she suggests meditation or medication, like they're my only options, when neither one makes my mom stay alive. I cry again on the drive home.

I avoid seeing the therapist again, ignoring her calls asking if I'd like to make another appointment. In some ways, I'm exactly the way I was two-and-a-half years ago. Except this time I know I'm running away from it all.

A week later Mom asks me to drive her to the Gap. I'm surprised, but eager to do something normal. Upon arriving, I instantly regret going out in public this way. Mom used to stride into the store confidently, like it was the one place in the world she actually had a sense of direction. Now, like a little old lady, she shuffles toward a rack of comfy pants. I know things are bad because the pants aren't on sale, and she wants to try them on anyway. I trail closely behind, half-expecting her to perform an accidental trust fall at any moment.

When we finally make it across the store, I'm relieved to find that no one's even manning the fitting room. Privacy, at last.

"Missy, why do I look this way?" Mom asks in her slow voice once we're in the dressing room. "It's not normal."

She looks hazily in the mirror at her naked distended belly, a result of the cancer, the chemo, the side effects, who knows what. I imagine her pancreas and liver swollen and wanting out.

"You look great, Mom," I protest lightly. "You notice it more than anyone else."

"Said like a daughter," she sighs, stepping into a powder blue cotton pant leg, holding my shoulders for balance. And then suddenly she's falling, passing out, ninety pounds of dead weight leaning on me.

"Mom!" I hiss, looking around helplessly at the dressing room cubicle's white walls and slatted door. I send mixed prayers to the saleswomen: please help me; please don't come in. I've spent the last two-and-a-half years keeping Mom's illness a secret from our gossipy Long Island town. If she leaves the Gap on a gurney, they'll talk for weeks. And all that effort to keep it private will have been for nothing. Or has it been for nothing this whole time? Eventually there will be an obituary and a funeral. Will I still try to hide it, even then?

A quick jerky movement, like a hiccup, erupts from the heap slumped on top of me. She's woken up, thank God. Mom places her other leg into the pants, and then ties the drawstring in a big loopy bow, unaware that she's been gone. I try to keep my voice light but it shakes anyway: "Those look good, Mom—let's try on the rest at home." In slow motion, she gets dressed and puts back on her dusty blue baseball cap. On the way to the register, she reaches for a few pairs of socks, too.

That night Laura and Shari drag me to a bar. A cover band plays while they bop around on the sticky floor, and I wish to be someone else, anyone else: a girl who's able to toss her head back and laugh and dance, not a care in the world.

I get home and Mom's asleep in my bed. I grab my journal and a pen and tiptoe to the bathroom, where I can sit on the worn gray rug on the floor and write in peace:

> *Sometimes I think God is waiting until the rest*
> *of our family is "ready" to let my mom die. But*
> *what qualifies as ready? Me having a boyfriend to*
> *lean on? Jordan having a girlfriend? Dad having…*
> *Right.*
> *The bottom line is that we will never be ready,*
> *so sometimes I wish she would just*
> *GO!*
> *GO!*
> *GO!*

Marisa / Sally

I no longer believe in "Once upon a time." The world of fairytales is over for me—the naïveté, happily ever after, etc. Life has just become too real and difficult. Sometimes, downright painful.

It's not just my back and stomach that hurts, it's my heart. I am heartbroken. I can no longer make plans or hope everything will work out for the best. I know my life is in God's hands—fate is what keeps me alive or sucks the life out of me. It all remains to be seen.

One thing I know, though. Although I feel I may be gypped of a very important part of my life, I have lived a wonderful life. I have the most wonderful husband and a super-terrific son and daughter. This cannot be taken away from me. This will always be mine.

CHAPTER 28
Miss and Mom

Marisa / Sally

Two days after wishing my mom would GO! GO! GO!, my terrible wish comes true.

It starts off as one of the best days I've had all summer. I take the train to New York City and meet my college friend Adena at Penn Station, and we take the subway downtown to Soho. She's been interning in the photo department of a New Jersey newspaper, and we compare notes—the lousy bosses, the missed opportunities, the desire to do more. As we exit the R train and walk upstairs into the bright August sunshine, for a moment I see us as if we're a photo in a magazine: two young, pretty girls chatting and giggling, the sun threading through our beautiful dark curls.

And, actually, it's our hair that brings us to the city. Adena has discovered a new salon, Devachan, that specializes in curly hair, and we've saved up all summer to try it. My stylist, a Brazilian man named Francis, offers me iced tea in a champagne flute and calls me "gorgeous" while Adena is whisked away by a woman with wonderful curls of her own. We wave goodbye-for-now excitedly. I never want to leave.

Over an hour later, I'm transformed into a glamorous woman with shiny, bouncy curls falling in layers to my shoulders. I feel pretty and mysterious as we exit the salon, thinking I could be anyone—an actress, a model, a famous writer. I am anonymous and free strolling down the sidewalk, just another pedestrian walking and shopping in the city. Adena and I stop to admire our reflections in a store window, adjusting a curly strand this way or that, gushing over each other's new looks.

Suddenly it's 2 p.m. and we're starving, searching for a café among a million clothing and furniture stores. My cell phone rings and when I see it's my dad, my heart quickens.

"Hello?" I ask nervously.

"Missy, hi. Listen…I need you to come home."

"What's wrong? Did something happen?"

"No…Mom's upstairs resting," he says. "Just come home. We'll talk then, OK?"

"OK."

Adena knows my mom is sick and understands my desperate, frenzied look, the rushed hug goodbye. The subway ride back to Penn Station and the Long Island Rail Road ride home take an hour and a half, but it feels like I can't get there quickly enough. I want to run alongside the train just so I'll constantly be in motion. Another part of me doesn't want to go home at all. I force myself to just not think, staring out the window, tapping out drumbeats with my fingers and heels, singing my favorite sad songs in my head.

I walk in the door and Dad ushers me through the kitchen into the den. I try asking questions, but he shushes me, not wanting to wake Mom upstairs. He sits at the kitchen table and I slip into my chair across from him, heart racing.

"Mom's dying," Dad says quietly, looking relieved to be able to tell someone.

"What? How do you know?" I demand.

"I took her for chemo earlier, and the doctor noticed her eyes were yellow, and her skin is turning yellow, too—jaundice."

"She's yellow?" I ask, incredulous.

"You'll see it now," he says. "Once they pointed it out to me, I couldn't believe we hadn't noticed."

"What does that mean—jaundice?" I ask.

"Her liver's shutting down, her major organs are shutting down," Dad says matter-of-fact. "They didn't even end up giving her the chemo."

Somehow that last line is the saddest. Mom was willing to be on chemo the rest of her life if it would prolong it. She was always researching new drugs, volunteering for experimental trials, willing to do whatever it took. I find myself hoping she still thinks she got the chemo today—the worst side effect of not getting it being sheer hopelessness.

"Did they say how long...?" I ask. My eyes fill.

"They don't know, Missy. It could be a few days, a week...that's why I told you to come home," Dad says. "She's sleeping now, but when she wakes up you should spend some time with her."

I touch my hair, self-consciously. I hate that I cut my hair today. I hate that I had a good day. I hate that I didn't see the clues—the yellow face and eyes.

"I called hospice," Dad continues. "A nurse is going to come by later to check on Mom."

The word *hospice* makes me shudder. I know from Grandma dying that hospice means the end. Make the patient comfortable. No more drugs, no more life-saving measures.

Dad hesitates, trying to form what he wants to say. Suddenly, I realize how hard this must be on him and notice the lines across his forehead, his pale complexion despite the summer, how his eyes look down and never quite meet mine—it would be too sad.

"I don't think we should tell Mom," he says carefully. "It'll only make her more anxious and depressed...I don't want to upset her."

I'm shocked. I want to argue, "No, we *have* to tell her." But I trust that Dad knows what he's doing, and the last thing I want to do is defy him and upset him further. I agree to keep it a secret—but I don't know how I'm going to. Mom is the person I tell when something's wrong. And now that the something wrong is her, I can't tell her. Who will teach me how to watch Mom die? And is it even fair to keep it from her; doesn't she have a right to know?

Hospice puts a hospital bed in Mom and Dad's room, next to their bed, so that Mom may rest more comfortably. While Mom dozes during the day, Jordan and I camp out on the faded blue carpet at the foot of her bed, his pit bull Sadie lying between us. We barely talk, but his simple nearness comforts me. Nothing's on TV, so we watch *American Pie 2*. Mom wakes occasionally, laughing randomly at all the wrong parts because she's trying so hard to keep up. During a particularly funny moment, she remarks, "This is really a sad movie." Jordan and I look at each other and try to hide our snickering, but she's already back asleep.

That night, I call Laura. She picks me up right away and we drive to the beach. We don't even get out to walk on the boardwalk; it would seem too cheerful. Instead I make her drive up and down streets named after states we've never been to—Kentucky, Missouri, Tennessee—as I confess that I have no idea what to do.

"Maris, I think you're doing everything you can do," she comforts me. She doesn't even complain about all the gas we're wasting, willing to drive me around for hours until the nerves kick in—*what if she's dying right now and you're at the fucking beach?*—and then she speeds to get me home.

I quit my internship a week early, feeling some satisfaction in telling my two obnoxious bosses that my mom is dying. They are the walking stereotype of marketing girls: shallow, gossipy, loud. An editorial girl like me—soulful, sensitive, quiet—was never going to fit in. On the first day, they selected one intern as their favorite and that was that. For the rest of the summer, they forced her to delegate menial tasks to the rest of us, removing the need to even exchange a hello with any of us lesser interns. They remind me of grown-up versions of the rich bitches from my high school. I only feel more validated when the news about my mom is met with plastic sympathy: "Oh Gawd! Sweetie, you shoulda told us sooner!"

Still, their words echo as I walk back to my drab cubicle. What would the summer have been like if I had told them sooner? Is it possible that even these cold-hearted women would have warmed to me, taken me under their wings, or at least said things like "Of course, sweetie!" if I'd asked to leave early to see Mom in the hospital instead of biting my nails until 5 p.m. on the dot? Why, two-and-a-half years later, was I still fighting so hard to keep Mom's illness a secret? When will I realize that hiding it from others doesn't make it go away?

The silver lining: that afternoon I finally get up the nerve to ask one of the magazine editors if I can help him with anything, thinking he'll let me make photocopies or transcribe an interview. I'm shocked when, instead, he assigns me a piece to write. My first published piece in a national magazine! It is a glimmer of hope for my future, a shiny strand of silver garland that I can touch and know things might be OK.

Hospice estimates Mom has a few days, but just as she outlived the two-month prognosis, she outlives the two-day prognosis, hanging on for nearly two weeks. The days continue to pass the same way for me—movies with Jordan during the day, out with friends at night. On one of her last days, an old Simon & Garfunkel concert on PBS has Jordan and me mesmerized, tears streaming noiselessly down our faces as we listen to "The Sound of Silence." Mom alternates between sleep and babbling about cats being spayed, but when I feed her or change her clothes she studies me with a soulful look and strokes my hand. I sense her trying to memorize me. I can't fully return the look, worried I'll break down and spill the secret that she's dying. It's the first and last secret I've kept from her, and I feel guilty every minute.

Other days friends and family from all over the country come to visit, sitting with Mom while she sleeps. I awkwardly entertain them with questions and stories, trying to be as charismatic and fun as Mom used to be. I long to make her dying less obvious and sad. It doesn't work; everyone cries.

Laura and Natalie pick me up one night to meet Natalie's childhood friend Karina at TGI Fridays. Just like Mom, I can't follow the conversation, can't laugh at the right moments. Instead I watch Karina—so pretty and sweet, her ponytail swinging cutely as she giggles at one of Natalie's sarcastic remarks. Laura eyes me watchfully. "Do you need to go home, Marisa?" she asks quietly. I nod tersely. They drop me off and continue on without me. Watching them drive away, I long to be with them and long to be without them.

One afternoon, Dad's downstairs and Jordan's napping, and I creep upstairs in search of a moment with Mom alone. She's dozing. I sit on the edge of her hospital mattress, ironically covered in the leopard-print college sheets she picked out for me two years ago. If anyone can make hospice hip, it's Mom. I pet them as I did in the store. The guilt is eating me alive, and I'm worried that if I continue to hide Mom's prognosis from her, I'll always regret it. Her eyes flutter open and settle on mine.

"Mom, do you know what's going on?" I ask gently.

She pauses, looking hazily at a faraway spot. When she responds, her voice is soft.

"Everyone's coming to visit," she says slowly. "I must be dying."

I don't agree or disagree, but it's enough to assuage my guilt, to feel that Mom knows there's not much time.

I swing my legs up onto the hospital bed and scooch down to lie beside her, head on her chest, arm wrapped around her waist. The comforting pose I've sought for the past twenty years. Mom covers my hand with hers.

I close my eyes and see a yellow house. It's a shack of a house, with beat-up children's toys splayed all over the front yard. I can't place it right away—is it from a memory, or a dream? And then finally I do place it: in the middle of nowhere in upstate New York. This house was my landmark when we'd drive Jordan to sleepaway camp each summer—the heads-up that camp was only a few minutes down the road. The sight of it would make my heart race as I strained my skinny nine-year-old neck to look back at it longingly through the rear windshield. It was the anticipation of having to say goodbye, of our family of four suddenly becoming a family of three.

All this time, for the past two-and-a-half years, I've been waiting for the yellow house—the sign that it's time to say goodbye to my mother. Instead I open my eyes and see yellow skin, yellow eyes, her yellow hand stroking my pink one. It's time to say what there is to say. Mom seems to sense this, too.

"You're a good kid, Miss."

A gentle whisper I'll remember my whole life. I make my tears have no sound, gulping down sobs. I pray my voice will be calm so she won't know it's goodbye.

"You're a good mom, Mom."

Epilogue

There's something about newborns that seems infinitely wise and connected to all that came before. Perhaps it's because babies, too, travel through darkness and into the light. In the days before my daughter is due, I wonder if birth and death are inextricably linked, and if my children get special protection in those wondrous moments pre-and post-birth. My mom, the true midwife into this world.

That's why I sense that when my daughter is born, the heaviness inside me will crack open and flood out. I will tell her everything. About my mom, about my loss, about the grief I have carried around. And yet, once my daughter is born, I say nothing of my mother. I'm wordless when the doctor places her on my chest, silent when I nurse her while the rain drips down our hospital window. I should have known that, just as with my son, I can't bear to burden her with my grief. Maybe she already knows everything. Maybe she truly knows nothing. I pet her puppy-soft dark hair and kiss her velvet cheeks and stroke the small of her back. And in the quiet with her, I feel understood.

I'm sent home from the hospital in time for Mother's Day. After many spent in misery, this one is a miracle. In our sunny Brooklyn apartment, I lay on the couch and hold my newborn daughter close, her tiny ear pressed against my swelling heart. Instead of telling her about my mom, I tell her about the kind of mom I long to be. With my silence, I show her that I will always listen. I whisper that she can tell me anything—no judgment, no criticism, not a peep. I remember all the times I went upstairs to my mother's room and lay quietly beside her until the words began to trickle out. I sense that, in the years to come, this is the only way my daughter, too, will reveal to me all the things deeply rooted in her heart.

The first time I cry while holding my daughter, she is three weeks old. I've just been told that my great aunt Ruthy—the one whose love and affection so closely mirror my mother's—is in the hospital. She is ninety-eight, yet I know it will always be too soon to lose her, that it will mean losing my mother all over again. Tears drip onto my daughter's dark hair, and I feel guilty for introducing her to my grief. But she doesn't fuss or cry. Instead she fixes her piercing navy blue eyes on me and, for the first time, reaches out and grabs my hand. I hold her gaze, transfixed. Did my mother feel this way when I looked at her, when I held her hand? Even in my worst moments as a teenager, even in her worst moments of illness, did my mere existence ease her sorrow? I've always known that daughters seek the comfort of their mothers; it's what I've been missing for years. But as my baby girl's fingers clutch my hand, I realize that mothers draw strength from their daughters, too.

My daughter won't know her Grandma Sally, not in the way she knows her Nana and Grammy and my stepmother Tippy. But my mom is not absent from this part of my story.

My son, at three years old, already knows about Grandma Sally. He has curled up in my lap to look at countless photos and watch old home videos. He's even placed stones on her grave. But, for a toddler, it's just rocks to collect and a grassy field to run around. He still seems too young to know what happened, or maybe I'm just not ready to hear her death come out of his mouth. I don't want him to know that mommies die.

With my daughter, it's simpler. Telling her about my mother requires no words; her presence is that near. She is my hands when I pet my daughter's hair. She is my heart beating into my daughter's ear. She is the very essence of who I long to be as a mother, and who I inevitably am. Most daughters cringe at the idea of becoming their mothers; I welcome the transformation. I only hope I'll be able to create the same indelible bond between mother and daughter. In sickness and in health. 'Til death do us part. The unspoken vows we solemnly swear to our children.

One day I'll tell my son and daughter the truth about my mother dying. I'll read some books and try to find the right words. I'll say it in a way that's gentle and loving and thoughtful, just as my mother would have done with me. I just need the courage to do it. Until then, I'll feed them her favorite fruits and recipes. I'll explain the world around them with her teacher's patience. I'll share her funny stories and hear her loud laugh in my own. I'll smother them with the endless love and affection she poured into me. For so long, my mother's death overshadowed all the memories that came before. Now, with my children, I get to share the best parts of my mother: the parts where she was alive.

Marisa Bardach Ramel
September 1, 2018

Acknowledgments

I started this book as a teenage daughter and ended it as a wife and mother. How do I begin to thank all the people who have entered my life over the past two decades? It's an impossible task. The list starts here and continues in my heart, where there is no word count to abide by.

Authors always save the best for last, but she deserves to be first: Sally Bardach. Mom, we may have only had twenty years, but your unlimited affection, real conversations, and belief in me have been enough to last a lifetime. Thank you for continuing to write this book with me for all these years, and for pulling strings from above when I needed you. May your memory live on in the hands of our readers.

After Sally died, my dad Bill Bardach stretched to become both Mom and Dad. As a parent now myself, I can't imagine the growing pains this involved, and yet he did it in his steady, calm way. Dad, you are truly an unsung hero, and you'll always be mine.

My brother Jordan Bardach requested I embellish this book by giving him celebrity girlfriends. J, thanks for making me laugh—through it all, together.

My mom believed the hole in our hearts would heal with love, and my life truly began again when I met my husband, Mark Ramel. Mark, your unwavering love and ridiculous sense of humor bring joy to my life in a way I once never thought possible. Thank you, too, for our beautiful book cover.

My son, Emmet, or, actually, the idea of him, was my motivation to finally finish writing this book, and his toddler fandom has been one of the most fun parts of publishing it.

My daughter, Willoughby, is proof that my mom is still smiling down on me. I'll always be thankful for you, my little doll.

The real-life Laura, Laura Hammond, deserves a medal for best friendship, as does my forever cheerleader Shari Silver. I wouldn't have made it without my college girls: Linda Mizel, Katie Benoit Cardoso, and Abigail Sessions. And to all the boys in the book, please know I wrote this with appreciation for our younger selves.

I'm forever grateful for Susan Bardach, who Emmet calls my "second mommy," a much sweeter—and truer—title than step-mother. My great aunts Ruth Sweedler and Shirley Hodes, ages 99 and 102, who make me believe I come from generations of writers. Gackie and Guckie, Susi Bardach, Julia Bardach, Sylvie Levine, and Deena Levine, all of whom lovingly watched my children so I could write. Sherry Rosen, Maxine Mintzer, Bonnie Horenstein, and Rose Giannetta, who shared memories of my mom. And Sharon Routt, my mother-in-law, who encouraged me to keep going.

No motherless daughter wants to admit she needs "other mothers," but Nancy Cleary at Wyatt-MacKenzie Publishing is just that, cheering me on with endless enthusiasm and warmth. At Thompson Literary Agency, Meg Thompson felt this book with her heart and Cindy Uh pushed me as a writer further than I ever thought I could go. The book never felt more truly seen than when it was in the hands of my editor, Kiley Frank (and ditto for an early edit by Sarah Saffian). Tracy Salcedo-Chourré copyedited with unique sensitivity, as she was the "Laura" to her best friend in high school; her work on this book is a tribute to the late Mrs. Haden. Karen V. Kibler bravely proofread the book just weeks after her own mother died. Gloria Dawson leaned over her pregnant belly to take copious grapefruit photos for the cover, while Melissa Thornton took the winning author photo simply by making me laugh. Kerri Kaplan, President & CEO of the Lustgarten Foundation for Pancreatic Cancer Research, generously wrote the foreword—and then told *everyone* about the book. Kerri, I love that you're spunky like Sally.

Many authors and editors generously offered support, including Cheryl Strayed; Hope Edelman; Allison Gilbert; Claire Bidwell Smith; Joy-Ann Reid, Will Schwalbe, Jill Santopolo; Joyce Raskin; Tré Miller Rodriguez; Erin Zammett Ruddy; Marika Roth; Rebecca Soffer and Gabi Birkner; Amy Newmark; Sara Lieberman; Denise Valenti; Jess Rozler; Cara Bedick. My editor-friends answered an absurd amount of questions: Katie Benoit Cardoso; Lara Asher; and Marisa Vigilante. The original writing group edited the book with tender hearts and wise hands: Beth Levine, Nancy Sun, and Lauren Kosa. Jennifer Zuccarelli gave it her promotional prowess. And the late, great Richard Kressler told me the first draft stunk long before any editor ever did.

Lastly, my gratitude to Howard Bruckner, MD of Bruckner Oncology and his former physician's assistant Jennifer Marino—you are the miracle workers who extended Sally's life so we could hold onto her a little bit longer, which enabled us to write this book.

CPSIA information can be obtained
at www.ICGtesting.com
Printed in the USA
LVHW090628070619
620481LV00001BA/162/P

9 781948 018364